GIRLS ALOUD
Dreams That Glitter

TRANSWORLD PUBLISHERS
61–63 Uxbridge Road, London W5 5SA
A Random House Group Company
www.rbooks.co.uk
First published in Great Britain in 2008 by Bantam Press, an imprint of Transworld Publishers
Copyright © Cheryl Cole, Nadine Coyle, Sarah Harding, Nicola Roberts and Kimberley Walsh, 2008

Every effort has been made to obtain the necessary permissions with reference to copyright material, both
illustrative and quoted. We apologize for any omissions in this respect and will be pleased to make the
appropriate acknowledgements in any future edition.
© Ian Bartlett: 97, 179, 219, 220–221, 235
© Rob Cable/Cableimage: 5, 8–9, 26, 29, 30, 34–5, 60–1, 74, 87, 91, 93, 94, 96, 98–9, 108, 128, 131, 132,
134, 141, 144–5, 172, 175, 176, 180–1, 184, 193, 194–5, 207, 213, 215, 217, 236–7, 238–9, 241, 249, 252
© Sarah Duthie: 68
© WireImage/Getty Images/Jon Furniss: 110–1
© Justin Goff/UK Press/PA Photos: 105
© Getty Images Entertainment/Getty Images/Claire Greenway: 136–7
© ITV plc: 11, 12, 13, 14, 16, 19, 22, 24, 37, 44, 51, 52, 65, 97, 134, 135, 179
© Ken McKay/Freemantle Media: 245
© OK! Magazine: 156
© Rex Features: 39, 81, 162, 179
© Ian West/PA Photos: 56
With thanks to Cheryl Cole, Nadine Coyle, Sarah Harding, Nicola Roberts and Kimberley Walsh,
Angela O'Connor, Liz Martin, Arthur Gourounlian: 32-3, 76, 96–7, 102, 113, 116, 119, 125, 134–5, 143,
152, 178–9, 189, 198, 203, 218–9, 224, 229, 231

Cheryl Cole, Nadine Coyle, Sarah Harding, Nicola Roberts and Kimberley Walsh have asserted their
rights under the Copyright, Designs and Patents Act 1988 to be identified as the authors of this work.

Project Editor: Helena Caldon
Design by Lynnette Eve / lynne@design-jam.co.uk

A CIP catalogue record for this book is available from the British Library.

ISBN 9780593061220 (hb) / ISBN 9780593061305 (pbk)

Addresses for Random House Group Ltd companies outside the UK can be found at:
www.randomhouse.co.uk
The Random House Group Ltd Reg. No. 954009

The Random House Group Limited supports The Forest Stewardship Council (FSC), the leading
international forest-certification organization. All our titles that are printed on Greenpeace-approved
FSC-certified paper carry the FSC logo.
Our paper procurement policy can be found at www.rbooks.co.uk/environment

Printed in Italy

6 8 10 9 7

GIRLS ALOUD

Dreams That Glitter

BANTAM PRESS

LONDON · NEW YORK · TORONTO · SYDNEY · AUCKLAND

We would like to say a HUGE thank you to our fans who have been unbelievable over the past six years. You have always been there and your constant support and belief in us has made this all possible. It is your letters and messages that keep us going through the more difficult times and we are so happy we can experience all the good times together too! We thank you from the bottom of our hearts for everything you do. We love ya! xxx

We would like to thank to say a special thank you to our families, partners and friends for helping us achieve our dreams. Thanks for always being there and keeping us sane throughout all the madness! We really don't know what we'd do without you. xxx

There are so many amazing and unbelievably talented people that have been a part of the Girls Aloud families over the years. Everyone listed below has been hugely involved in our career so far, and has helped us to grow and achieve more than we could have ever dreamed of. We have come a long way and could never have enough words to thank you all. Glad you could all share this incredible journey with us. xxx

Hillary Shaw, Angela O'Connor, Lily England, David Joseph, Colin Barlow, Peter Loraine, Poppy Stanton, Rachel Cook, Claire Mitchell, Pippa Evers, Brian Higgins, Miranda Cooper, Sundraj Sreenivasan, Drew Lyall, Beth Honan, Lisa Laudat, Liz Martins, Victoria Adcock, Frank Strachan, Solomon Parker, Sheraz Qureshi, Toby Leighton-Pope, Iain Whitehead, Jeremy Hewitt, Richard Bray, Robyn Bradshaw, Alan McEvoy, Rob Cable, Kenny Ho, Paul Roberts, Chloe Richardson, Chloe Butcher, Pat Lomax.

Finally, our deepest gratitude to Maria Malone for her friendship, warmth and endless patience and to Sarah Emsley for helping us create something we can keep forever. We are eternally grateful.
All our love, xxx

The lights go down in the arena. Images flash across giant screens either side of the stage. In the darkness, suspended on wires high above the audience, we're on the verge of a show that will mark another milestone for us as a band. Below, the dancers are in position, the band is ready. Our names echo around the venue. The atmosphere is charged, electric; we can all feel it. Just seconds from now the curtains will open. Those final few moments bring a powerful rush of emotion and excitement.

The haunting sound of a choirboy's voice fills the air, the cue for an explosion of music and light, as the curtains open.

There are 15,000 people in the house. They're there just for us and they're on their feet, going mad. The sound of clapping and screaming is deafening. For us, looking out across the vast arena, it's a breathtaking sight, overwhelming. This is what we always dreamed of, what we love most about being Girls Aloud, and this is the most dramatic entrance we've ever made. We glance at each other in our futuristic costumes, capes fanning out behind us, hair lifted by the giant wind machines beneath us, and it's as if we really are flying.

It's Friday 16 May 2008, almost halfway through the 'Tangled Up' tour, and we're about to play our biggest ever gig at the 02 Arena in London.

As we're lowered to the stage – even before we launch into 'Sexy! No No No …' – we're on the biggest high ever because we know we're in for yet another magical night.

Six years ago the five of us hadn't even met. What brought us together was the dream we shared to be pop stars. Five normal girls, all with the same burning ambition to be up there on stage, singing and performing: it was the only thing any of us ever wanted.

Like thousands of other hopefuls, we spent hours queuing at venues around the UK, in 2002, to take part in a new reality TV show. We'd done our share of auditions before, had our setbacks and disappointments, but this time was going to be different.

This time, our lives were about to change forever.

Since then, we've been on the most amazing journey together and achieved so much more than we ever dreamed possible. We still have moments when we can't quite believe just how far we've come, that this extraordinary life really is ours.

We'd love our story to inspire you to have faith in your dreams, whatever they might be, and to go for them, no matter what.

We won't pretend getting to where we are today has been an easy ride, but, whatever the ups and downs, our fans have always been there, through the good times and the not-so-good times. We can't even begin to put into words how much it means to us to have your constant love and support and to know you're sharing this whole adventure with us. We're so grateful to you.

We'd like to dedicate this book to all those who believed in us and encouraged us to believe in ourselves.

With love and thanks,

Cheryl, Kimberley, Nadine, Nicola and Sarah.

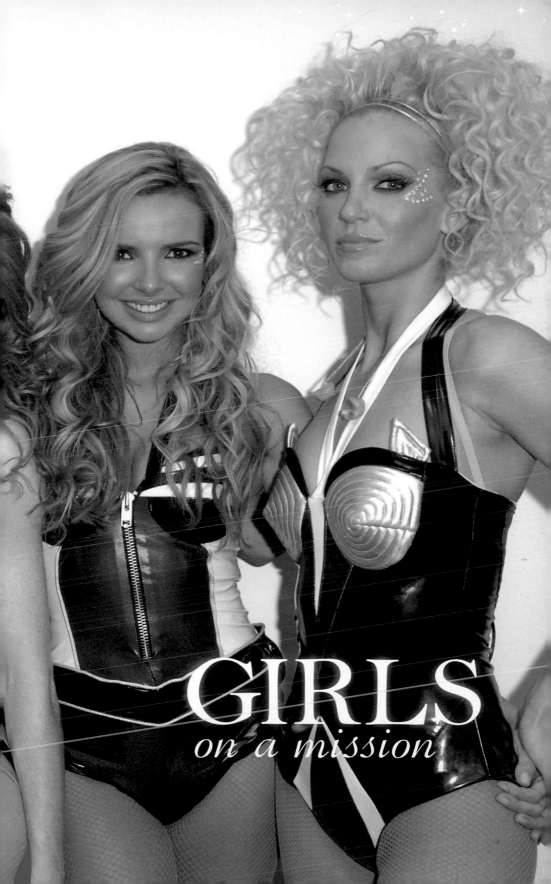

GIRLS
on a mission

Summer 2002. Across the UK thousands of hopefuls audition for a new ITV reality show called *Popstars: The Rivals*. The aim: to create two bands – one girls, one boys – who'll go head to head for the Christmas number one. Just 20 hopefuls will make it through to the final stages of the competition where they will perform live on prime-time television each week, and the viewers will vote to keep their favourites in the running. First, though, they face an intense audition process that only the strongest will survive.

CHERYL: I was always one of those people who said I would never go on a reality TV show, but when the advert came on for *Popstars: The Rivals* I was really low, the lowest I could possibly get, and I just thought, what have I got to lose by sending off for an application form?

Ever since I was a kid I'd loved performing, being on stage, singing and dancing and showing off. There was just always something inside of me, almost like I knew that was my destiny, like there was no other option. I never had a Plan B, something I'd do just in case; I was on this one track wanting to perform. When I was a teenager, though, I went through a really horrible and unconfident stage. I think in general your teenage years are like that because you're not a child any more, not quite a woman, and you're learning about yourself, but I'd also been in a terrible relationship for two years.

Before I did the audition in 2002 I'd been clinically depressed and dangerously underweight. I was having terrible panic attacks and suffered from anxiety, and as a result my appetite went. Any food used to make my stomach churn. I was 5 stone 11 pounds at my worst point, like a walking corpse, basically. A lot of things had happened: I'd lost a friend, a boy I'd known for years, who'd overdosed on heroin, and another friend of mine was stabbed and killed – over drugs again – and left two children behind. For two years I was in a really destructive relationship, where the guy I was with had seen what I'd been going through, losing people, and was using drugs behind my back and lying about it. There was a lot of stuff going on so I went to the doctor and had counselling and was given antidepressants. I was really poorly, mentally, and for a long time I wouldn't go out of the house, I just wanted to be indoors with the curtains closed.

It was actually my mother who packed up all my stuff and made me come home, and that's when I saw the advert for *Popstars: The Rivals*. I remember telling my little brother to watch for it to take down the number and when he switched channels just seconds later the advert was on. We were both so freaked out we started screaming and missed the number.

I auditioned in London, went down the night before and stayed in a hotel. I'd bought a new outfit in Newcastle thinking I looked fine, but when I look back I don't know what I was thinking. I didn't really have a clue about style and I wasn't one of those teenagers that read all the magazines and followed fashion. I just did my own thing. I got what I could with what money I had at the time: a flowery top, a cross-choker necklace, and trousers with tiny little checks and a pleat down the front. I was just 19 and singing in front of the judges was quite tough for me. I've never been so scared in all my life. I really wanted it but I had a lot of insecurities and I had these three powerful people watching me. Geri Halliwell had been in the Spice Girls so she knew everything about what we were letting ourselves in for, Pete Waterman was just about the biggest music mogul of the eighties, and Louis Walsh just made you think of Westlife and Boyzone. They were big chiefs. I sang S Club's 'Have You Ever' and I was shaking, just terrified, and I could hear it in my voice. I can't watch it back because it makes me feel quite ill and I can't believe I got through, the state I was in, but that gave me a little boost.

NICOLA: I was only 16, and I'd literally just left school, only

done my GCSEs a few weeks before the audition. I think it was my mum who'd seen the advert for the programme on the telly, and we got a form. I'd done a couple of demos in a local studio so we sent those off with it.

We were in Cornwall on a little caravan site on holiday when I got told to come for the audition and I was like, you are joking. My poor dad had to drive me to Manchester, me nervous as hell going through the song, Shakira's 'Underneath Your Clothes', in the car all the way there, and my dad going, 'You better get in, now.' When we got there we couldn't find the hotel, couldn't find anywhere to park, it was the biggest stress, then we saw the queue and it was so long it was an absolute joke. I remember seeing Kimberley and she looked really pretty and bronzed and glowing.

I've always been really confident with my singing, but when I went in to see Louis and Geri and Pete I felt like I was really on the spot. All of a sudden I was in front of these famous people. When I was little Geri Halliwell was my biggest idol. She was just sitting there smiling and I didn't want to speak because I didn't know what to say. I sang and they were all really nice and put me through to the next stage in London. Then my dad drove us all the way back to Cornwall.

KIMBERLEY: I always wanted to sing, just had the
complete bug for performing. I'd done bits of TV and had quite a few near misses, like a TV show with Kelli Young where we'd played in a pretend band, which was ironic because that was before she did *Popstars* and got into Liberty X. I'd also got down to the last three for the part of Maria in *Coronation Street*, up against Samia Ghadie, who got it, and Suzanne Shaw, who also did *Popstars* and was in Hear'Say. I was thinking I should have gone for that

but I hadn't really known about it until it was too late, so when *Popstars: The Rivals* came round I thought I might as well have a go. I'd done lots of auditions but this one was really scary and I didn't know if I was going to be able to hold my nerve. I'd sent off a tape and a picture and they'd whittled down the numbers from something like 30,000 to 10,000 across the country and I was thinking I'd have a proper time slot for the audition, but when I got to Manchester there were loads of people waiting. I was stood in the queue for four hours, but luckily my mum was with me, and my sister, so they kept nipping off for drinks and stuff. I remember seeing Nicola in the queue and she had such a striking look, she really did stand out to me. Her hair was literally down to her bum.

I had a really good mindset that day. I just wanted to get through, to find out if there was some point in me carrying on. I was 20 and

I needed to hear it from people who knew what they were talking about. I sang Whitney Houston's 'Where Do Broken Hearts Go?', and when they put me through to the next stage I was just so glad.

SARAH: I was on the karaoke all the time, doing the circuit round Manchester, entering competitions to get over my nerves. I was always having near misses – almost getting into bands, half making it – but I'm glad I didn't now. A friend of mine, a writer and musician, wanted to start a girl group and auditioned some other girls to join me. We called ourselves Project G and went into the studio to record some stuff, but nothing really came of it. Then they let two of the girls go and kept me and one of the others on. She was doing more pop and I was recording dance tracks. We were on the verge of doing something with it when a friend said *Popstars* was coming and did I want to do it? I was 20, and I was like, hell no, I'm not going to make an idiot of myself in front of millions of people. I just didn't know if I could do it, but the night before the auditions I was chatting to an ex-boyfriend and it was playing on my mind and he was saying, what have you got to lose? Nothing but my pride, my dignity, everything … but he was right. So I rang my friend and we went down about one in the morning and joined the queue in front of the Lowry Hotel in Manchester. There were about 50 people in front of us and we had flasks of coffee, blankets and chocolate biscuits. I had my camcorder and got loads of stuff, so that's really nice for me to look back on. In the morning we saw Davina and Geri walking in. I didn't get seen until nearly midday and by then I was sweating and feeling horrible and crispy and dirty. They lined up 10 of us in a room to sing in front of the TV people and someone from the record company – that's the bit they don't show on telly – and if you're good enough or bad enough or interesting enough you go through to Louis, Pete and Geri.

I got through the first stage and I was going to sing 'I'll Be There', a big ballad, but Davina was walking up and down saying to make sure we had a back-up song. My mind went blank and all I could think of was Steps' 'Last Thing On My Mind'. I'd done auditions in the past and failed miserably because of my nerves, blanked and lost the key, and it was horrible thinking this is on TV now. It wasn't my best performance, because of my nerves, but I think they liked the fact I was a little bit crazy and outrageous. I definitely didn't get through purely on my singing. I stopped at McDonald's on my way home, so happy I'd got through, but trying to hold it down because my friend didn't and she was really deflated. I was thinking, God, this could change my life.

NADINE: I'd been through the whole Irish *Popstars* experience a few months before and I'd got into the band, but I was actually too young. So that was the end of that. Louis (Walsh)

had phoned me and told me to audition for *Popstars: The Rivals* but I was like, 'No, I don't want to do another TV show.' I'd been doing some showcases for solo things in Ireland and I felt I didn't want to be on my own, that I was too young, too afraid: just nervous that I didn't know what I was doing. I actually wanted to be in a band. Louis was managing a girl band called Bellefire and I said to him that's what I wanted, to have other girls around me, so he thought *Popstars: The Rivals* was perfect.

My boyfriend Neil's sister, Laura, wanted to audition and I'd been helping her with her singing. She asked me to go with her to Glasgow, so I did, but I wasn't going to audition, then when I got there I just thought I might as well. I met a couple of people I knew from Ireland and just thought, okay, you only live once, what's there to lose? So that was it. I sang Eva Cassidy's 'Fields of Gold' and I got through to the next stage in London. Neil's sister didn't get through, but she was fine, really happy for me.

CHERYL: I knew that the next stage where you auditioned for seven days and did different things, dancing and whatever, was going to be the clincher and I was kind of going through it all on my own. My mam loves me to bits and wishes me the best, but she's the most unenthusiastic person you could meet. I could hear other people's mothers screaming down the phone at each new stage they got through to, but I never had that. I'd ring her and say I'd got through and she'd say, 'Oh, that's good.' My dad was always telling me to get my head out of the clouds and go to college, that every teenage girl wants to be a pop star, so I was just thinking, you know what, I'm going to prove to all of you I can do this.

People always seem to assume I'm outgoing, but I can be quite shy, so the week of auditions in London was quite difficult. I got on with the girl I shared a room with but she went after the first night so I just tried to mingle the best I could. But it was nerve-racking. I remember seeing Kimberley and thinking she was stunning and I went over and said, 'Oh my God, you're so pretty, your skin is amazing.' She was like, 'Oh thanks, it's such-and-such foundation,' and I was thinking, I wonder what that is? I'd worn eyeliner and mascara and stuff but nobody in my family wore foundation and I thought maybe I could get some. I remembered Nadine from the Irish *Popstars* – I'd seen her talking about it on *CD:UK* – and I just thought Nicola was so striking and so shy and really pleasant. Scousers tend to have a lot of similar traits to Geordies so we really clicked. And Sarah, I just remember thinking she was a lunatic, one of those out-there girls, crying all the time. She had a big personality and she really stood out.

NADINE: I remember thinking Cheryl was really quiet and meek and softly spoken. I thought Sarah was a nutcase, crazy blonde, and that Kimberley was really sweet. I went up to her and said, 'I really like your trousers, where did you get them?' And that was it, we just started chatting. Nicola, she was really skinny with this strong Liverpool accent. I was 17, just a few months older, but I just remember thinking she looked how I felt: young and out of her depth.

NICOLA: I was just a baby, really young, quite shy as well, from this little town, Runcorn, and I didn't really have much life experience. It was the first time I'd been to London and I had my mum there because I was only 16. We checked into the hotel in Kensington and the next day everyone was taken to this massive hall with a stage, loads of cameras set up, hundreds of chairs, and we all had to go up on stage one by one and sing in front of everyone. It was like being thrown in at the deep end. I had Kimberley sitting next to me and she was practising and I was trying to help her, saying which bit of the song showed her voice off. I knew what I was going to sing and I was prepared and confident in my singing ability, but I was nervous about singing in front of everybody and the judges. When I walked up on the stage I didn't smile or nothing, I was just so terrified. Then Geri said, 'I think you're great, you're an individual, you really stand out,' so I knew she was on my side.

> 6 I was nervous about singing in front of the judges . . . Then Geri said, "I think you're great, you're an individual, you really stand out," so I knew she was on my side. 9

Obviously, I'd sat there and watched everybody sing and I didn't feel like, oh, they're all better than me. I thought I'd be okay and I actually wasn't all that scared, but at that time I didn't realize it was all about personality and the way you looked as well. Everybody seemed to have been at stage school – they knew how to work the camera and be all bubbly – and I was not like that at all. I was like this sad little fish, completely out of water.

There were people with full hair extensions and their nails done and tans and a new outfit every day, and we didn't have that kind of money. I was just in my trackies and I didn't have my nails done, didn't know anything about make-up or fake tan, so I must have looked a bit of a scruff. I was such a teenager and I wasn't old enough to think okay, that's how I need to work it, and come up with a plan. I didn't know how to play the game. I wasn't thinking, I need to be like them – be like what? Half the time I was petrified because I was shy so I wasn't smiling and Louis used to say, 'You need to smile more.' I felt like saying, I don't know anybody – what do you want me to do?

I kept getting through every day and I just tried to stay focused. When it got down to the last 15 I'd figured out it was to do with a lot more than singing. It was also about who had the biggest personality. I started to think I should be in the final 10 because, technically, I was a better singer than a lot of the people there, but I knew I didn't have the other side, that I wasn't a bubbly character. I remember the night we were leaving there was a bit of a party and everyone got drunk and one of the guys making the programme said to my mum that I wasn't that big a personality so they'd probably go for a girl who was a terrible singer but would make great TV. My mum was like, 'How can he say that?' But it's all politics, as horrible as it is.

NADINE: I remember being so nervous, just permanently, every day. I was constantly rundown and my mind was working overtime. I kept thinking, what's the worst-case scenario? I don't get in the band and end up back home. That's not so bad. But it just seemed there was so much pressure, suddenly being thrown into an adult world and having to act responsibly. The most I'd had to think about before was getting up for school. It was mind-boggling.

You become really friendly with people and you really care and then they were going, their dreams crushed right in front of you, and that's something that plays on your mind. There were people who'd been doing it for years, done every class, been for every audition, and they were getting thrown out. It was awful, and when you see people really hurting you almost think, my God, it wouldn't be so bad if it was me going. I don't like watching shows like *The X Factor* now when they're doing the early auditions because it just brings back such bad memories. It's so harsh. The judges are so cruel for the sake of TV.

KIMBERLEY: London was really intense for me. I don't think I'd anticipated how hard it would be because I felt I was used to the whole audition process and having knock-backs, but it was much more than a normal audition and I found it really hard to take. There were 50 of us to start with and the first thing they asked us to do was get up and sing in front of everyone and you just feel like it's a clincher, that whatever comes out of your mouth is going to determine whether you stay, and it was overwhelming. It was about putting on a front, making it seem you are confident even when you aren't and hoping you'll get through. I did, but it's emotionally draining and disappointing when you don't do your best and I think that can knock your confidence, which is what happened to me. Nerves were affecting my voice and I knew I wasn't doing myself justice. Even if you got through to the next day they'd give you a lot of negative comments, obviously trying to make you step up, and it just made me feel worse knowing I had to somehow do better. The nerves were out of control and I was feeling more and more terrified. The further along I got the less confident I was, and there was one day when you had to go in to see Louis, who was the girls' mentor, to find out if you were in the last 15, and he said I was through but I'd have to do better. That night I couldn't stop crying. I didn't know what was wrong with me; it was like something had triggered this emotion and I couldn't control it. Everyone was saying I'd be fine but I just knew

I wouldn't get through to the last 10. I was in a really weird state of mind; I couldn't stop crying and I don't usually cry that easily.

CHERYL: I was really emotional that week, one minute feeling happy and thinking wow, this is amazing, then just being so nervous and unsure of myself and crying my eyes out, not knowing why the hell I was putting myself through it and wondering if it was the right thing to do: just lots of different emotions. I loved meeting people, and every different character you could think of was there, but there was a lot of pressure and the further you got the more difficult it was. I felt I was getting closer, but every day I thought I could be gone.

We had to go in and see Louis one by one to find out if we were through to the last 15 and there were still two people to go in front of me and I could feel this horrible burning sensation inside. I just burst into tears and I was sobbing uncontrollably and didn't want to go in. If the answer was 'No' I didn't want to know. Why would I? The camera crew were saying, 'Stop it, you've got to pull yourself together,' but I was just so overwhelmed by everything that had gone on during the week that I couldn't. It was crunch time and I really thought he was going to say I wasn't ready mentally, or that I wasn't strong enough vocally.

> When he said I was through I cried. I couldn't stop . . . I lay in my room thinking, this is serious now; this could be me living my dream.

When he said I was through I still cried. I couldn't stop. When I got back to the hotel I was just exhausted from it all, totally drained. I rang my mam and she was, 'Oh good.' Totally unenthusiastic. Now she says it's because she wasn't surprised; she knew I could do it. I just lay in my room thinking, this is serious now; this could be me living my dream.

SARAH: I just kept thinking I wouldn't get through to the next round because it was dancing and I can't dance and I just blanked. You can see me on the programme trying to learn

the routine, spending loads of time with the dance coach; the music comes on, the judges are watching and I just can't do it. I got upset and Geri came over and was encouraging me, saying, 'Come on, you can do it.' I'd always found it hard to absorb routines as quickly as other people who've had training and I think maybe Geri empathized. Bizarrely, I still managed to get through so they must have seen potential somewhere. Every day I just thought I'd wing it, see what happens. I didn't want to set myself up for disappointment so I always expected the worst, then when I got through it was a nice surprise.

NADINE: I remember Louis coming to see me at home and my mammy, who's obsessed with cleaning anyway, had the whole place turned upside down because a camera crew was coming and they were going to be filming. I remember cleaning and the place looking no different because it was already clean.

I thought I'd done really well getting that far but I wasn't a dancer – I'd still say I'm not, but at least I can throw a shape at it now – and at the auditions we were given all these moves and people who'd been doing it for years were picking it up so quick and I hadn't got a clue so I thought, fair enough, I can sing but if they want dancers I won't get in. Louis said I was going to have to work on that but I'd got through to the final 10. I was really shocked; I couldn't believe it.

CHERYL: We had to wait two weeks to find out if we'd made it into the final 10 and Geri came to see me at home to tell me the answer and did this whole rambling speech before she said I was in. Getting into the *Popstars: The Rivals* house with the other nine girls made me think that maybe I wasn't as bad as I thought I was. I still have those moments now when I feel totally unconfident, but back then I was thinking my God, I have to step up now. We had to sing live on the show every week and I don't know how I did that. I'd never actually sung live in front of anyone before, not even sung karaoke.

KIMBERLEY: I did know deep down I wouldn't be in the last 10, because the nerves had got the better of me, and I told my family so they were prepared. Then Pete Waterman came to my home and said I wasn't through and I was like, 'Yeah, I know, I've got my head round it already,' but obviously that doesn't make good TV so he kept pushing me and I could see my mum getting upset and eventually I broke down. I felt worse for everybody else really because they'd been on this journey with me and seen me get nothing out of it. It was awful.

NICOLA: They had to pick the final 10 girls and Pete Waterman came to my house and he was like, 'I'm sorry, you haven't made it.' It was so strange because I really wasn't devastated. I had a feeling something was going to happen and then I got a call two weeks later to say one of the girls had moved out. They'd put a girl who was heavily pregnant into the *Popstars: The Rivals* house. I think she was due to give birth when the series was on air. So one of the researchers called and said, 'Geri's fighting for you, Pete's fighting for you, but Louis wants Kimberley.' I had to watch a programme with Louis Walsh saying why he didn't want me. Watching that programme gave me an insight as to how the industry works; the auditions made it clear that getting on in the industry would be a battle. They picked Kimberley and she went into the house, but I still felt like it wasn't the end of the world. I still had a feeling something would happen.

KIMBERLEY: I'd just accepted things. I thought it was the story of my life. There'd been loads of times I'd got close to something and ended up just missing out. Before the auditions, I'd been doing a degree in English and Media and was getting ready to go back to college in Leeds. Then I got a call to do a follow-up

interview, which turned out to be a set-up to tell me I was going into the house to replace Hazel, who was pregnant. Literally that day I'd registered for my third year at uni.

NICOLA: My mum heard from one of the boys' mums saying it had all kicked off and one of the girls hadn't signed the contract. I got a phone call from ITV2 asking me to go on a show for an interview and I just knew something was happening. We got picked up in a car and driven to London and I said to my mum, 'I will get into the house now.' She didn't want me getting my hopes up but I just knew. I had a feeling. So when they said someone's left and we're putting you in I was like, thank God! It was a big fingers up to Louis who didn't want me because I wasn't a big enough profile, a big-enough personality, or whatever, but I knew as soon as I was given an opportunity to sing every week, if I could just show everyone what I could do, there was a good chance I would make the band. Not to sound big-headed – I just believed in my vocal ability and it was something I was really passionate about.

CHERYL COLE

FULL NAME
Cheryl Ann

BORN
30 June 1983, in
Newcastle-upon-Tyne

STYLE
Honest, intuitive,
compassionate

INTO
Music, dance, performing

CAN'T STAND
Liars, celebrity columnists

SHE SAYS
'There's no such thing as
coincidence. I believe in
fate and I believe Girls
Aloud were meant to
be together. That's why
we've lasted.'

CHERYL: I grew up on a council estate in Newcastle; it wasn't unhappy but it was tough, very tough. It's not really until the last couple of years I've realized it wasn't as easy as a lot of people have it, but I'm not ashamed of it and I don't regret anything. I am who I am because of what I went through and I'm just grateful for what I've achieved. We didn't have any privileges. I remember living on baked beans and eggs and bread – if it wasn't out of date. It was, like, what are we having? Beans. Again. Fish fingers.

I've always been my own person, always known what I wanted to do. My mam says when I was four if I was having my photograph taken I'd be saying which way I wanted to pose and telling my dad – do one like this, or this would look better. I was always like that and I think that came from having older siblings and getting less attention. I was fourth in line. My eldest brother, Joseph, would have been seven when I was born and then Andrew was four and Gillian was five, only a year's difference between them, so they were like twins, like glue. By the time I was walking and talking they were doing their own thing and I was showing off to try and get attention. It was, 'Look at me – I'm dancing. Look!' I just had my own character and my own independence.

I've always been sensitive and put other people first, maybe because coming from a big family you have to compromise. If my little brother, Garry, needed new shoes then I'd wait a bit longer for mine. I remember at school somebody had lost his bus fare and he lived really far away and I gave him 25p, my bus fare, which was all I had, and I walked home. He never even said thank you, and it made me think that sometimes you're not better thought of or appreciated for trying to be the better person, and that sometimes you have to step back and do what's best for you. People can take kindness for weakness.

I'm glad I wasn't brought up in a privileged situation because you see some kids where all they've known is expensive clothes and getting all the latest models of this and that, and to me that's not experiencing life. If we got a McDonald's or a Chinese takeaway, oh my God, that was a treat, a luxury, because it was costing my mother a fortune. We used to get a Barbie that was four years out of fashion from a girl in the street who didn't want it any more. I'd get hand-me-downs from a girl up the road who had everything she wanted and she'd be like, 'Ha ha, Cheryl's got my jumper on.' I had all that rubbish, but I'm glad I've had the ups and downs and I'll definitely let my children know that life's not a bowl of cherries and, yes, you might have wonderful things, but believe you me you're going to appreciate them. There's no way they'll get everything they want. I'm glad me and Ashley come from that background because there's nothing worse than spoiled children. When we were little if we went to someone's house and touched an ornament we'd get our hand smacked. It was, 'Sit down, this is not your house. You can't run round like you can at home.' That's how it was. You go to people's houses now and there's somebody's kid drawing on their furniture and it's like, 'Don't do that, give mammy the pen.' We would have been given a smack and told to sit still.

I was brought up to be honest and I hate liars. My mother always said honesty is the best policy, which was probably her way of getting five kids to tell the truth, but it really stuck with me. I'd want my kids to be truthful and grounded and to realize that no matter what situation you're in, someone somewhere is worse off. I won't have a child that moans because they have to walk down the road. We had to walk to school every day. When I have kids I'll want them to realize they're very fortunate and it's not like that for everybody.

I think I'm ready for parenthood now. I wouldn't mollycoddle my kids or wrap them in cotton wool but I would be very aware of what they were taking in. When I was growing up my brother used to glue-sniff, which sounds like nothing now, but it was disturbing as a child. I remember I'd be sitting until five, six in the morning sometimes, watching at the window to see if he was coming down the street, just to check he was safe, then he'd come in and the whole house would smell of glue. Still, now, if I smell glue I get a funny feeling in my tummy.

There were quite a lot of kids at my school whose parents weren't together. Some kids hadn't even met their dad. I was one of the lucky ones and I was grateful I had 11 years of my mam and dad together before they split up. When they did there was a lot going on and I found a lot out at one go. I found out my mam and dad had never been married and that the older three weren't my biological brothers and sister, they were from my mam's first marriage, so nothing was how I'd thought it was. It was a whole hoo-ha and a lot to take in at that age.

As a child we didn't have any money and that made me fiercely independent. I like not having to rely on anyone. I was always a show-off but my goal in life was never to be famous, else I'd have gone on *Big Brother*. I was never someone who bought magazines every week or ever read the tabloids. The only time I'd even really see a magazine was at the doctor's or at the dentist's, and even then they were like two years old or something. My goal was to show people I can succeed in what I love to do. I feel like I'm meant to be doing this and I love it. Fame is just something that comes with it. Sometimes you get perks of the job when someone sends you free jeans because you wore a pair in a magazine, then there's the bad side where they take shots of your knickers and all that nasty business, but ultimately I make a good income and I have a gorgeous home and I'm grateful for my life. I'm a million times stronger than my mother. She was only 17 when she had her first child and then she had another four and never really experienced the nice things in life, so now I like to spoil her. She looks up to me and comes to me for advice. It's like role reversal at times, quite weird.

Q&A

Q How would you sum up your attitude to life?
A Live each day as it comes and don't take anything too seriously.

Q Do you have a favourite place?
A Newcastle means a lot to me. It's where I'm from and I just get a good feeling when I go back home. Sun-wise, Thailand's beautiful and the people are really nice.

Q If you're feeling low, how do you raise your spirits?
A Music, definitely. It's always my answer. If you're feeling low and you put on a good album you can't go wrong really; it picks your spirits up. Mary J. Blige and Alicia Keys are my favourites. They make me feel better and I sing along. Music can change people's lives. It totally touches you. It helps you heal heartache, helps you through losing someone; it can make you happy when you're sad. I wouldn't get out of bed if music didn't exist. There'd be no point in living – I feel that strongly.

Q Any phobias?
A Cotton wool. I hate cotton wool. I went to the dentist the other day and he put it in my mouth and I felt violated for the whole day. I never use it, not for taking make-up off or anything. Even when I get my nails done they use tissues. Just the feel of it…. it squeaks. Urgh. I can't bear it.

Q What's your favourite food?
A I think your tastes change anyway as you get older, and mine have 100 per cent. I would never have eaten an olive; I used to think, why would anyone choose to eat them? Now I love them. I hated fish and seafood and now I'll eat smoked haddock, cod and shrimp. I eat vegetable sushi and I've tried rock shrimp but I soak it in soy sauce. I've got a real thing about salt: I put it on everything. I love tempura, miso soup, and edamame beans. Before I would eat takeaways, fish and chips, frozen foods, and shop at places like Netto or Morrisons. It was all fish fingers and chips, beans and chips, egg and chips … all that kind of stuff. My gran used to cook chips in lard and they were the best. I didn't really eat out much because I couldn't afford to. For my eighteenth I went to a Chinese buffet where you could eat as much as you wanted for £5.

Q How do you unwind?
A When I get in at night I have a shower, put my pyjamas on and watch TV – the soaps and trashy American shows I shouldn't really admit to, like *Maury* and *Ricki Lake*. I find cooking really therapeutic but I'm not great at it. I'm learning.

CHERYL

In the *Popstars: The Rivals* house, a mansion on a private estate in Surrey, the finalists push themselves to the limit to turn their dreams of pop stardom into reality. Life will never be the same for the five who make it into the band and land a record deal. As they prepare for a gruelling series of live TV shows that will see one girl eliminated each week, the strain begins to show.

NADINE: I was excited about going to London and being in the last 10 in the house but I was a long way from home and I didn't have my family around me, which I'd always had, and we were doing a lot of work, a lot of important stuff every day. It was mentally draining and I just kept getting ill, coming out in cold sores with the stress. It was just being so worried and scared all the time, knowing you had a live show to do and that you had to get the song right. And because you're so busy you have no time to think, oh God, I've got another cold sore, I can't open my eyes I'm so tired. I was just so rundown. My mum was really worried because she was so far away. I think she cried more than I did. Then I found a lump in my breast. I was getting so ill and rundown I thought maybe it was all connected. My sister had been through the same thing with a lump in the same place, and had to have an operation to have it removed, so it was scary. A doctor came to the house, then I went to see someone in Harley Street, and as a young girl, just 17, having a doctor tell you to take off your top and your bra just felt like, 'Oh my God, I am in hell. This can't get any worse.' I'd always been prudish anyway, even getting changed in front of stylists made me really uncomfortable, and I just had that self-conscious thing of being so young. The doctor said there was definitely a lump and referred me to hospital for an ultrasound scan. Basically, it was a case of wait and see. If nothing comes back cancerous it's maybe just lymph nodes and it might disappear in time. It did go through my mind it might be cancer.

When the doctors were saying yes, there is something, and the T people were allowing me to take a week off, I knew it was serious. We couldn't even get a five-minute break and they were giving me a week off, so they had to be worried.

Then the results came back clear and everything was fine and as I started to feel better about my health generally it just kind of disappeared, and I haven't had any trouble since. That was the worst time for me but I think it was more scary for my family because they were so far away.

I'm sure loads of women go through those scares but I thought I had to get it checked out, even though it was just something small. With these things it's better to know sooner rather than later, and now I'll just keep an eye out and monitor myself. My advice to anyone would be to get over the embarrassment factor, as that should be nothing when it comes to your health.

Stress is extraordinary. It's strange what it can do, how it can make you feel so bad. I have a great mental attitude to work and I think my mind could deal with everything that was going on but my body couldn't. I'd feel I just couldn't get out of bed in the morning. I was sharing a room with Kimberley and she'd be up getting ready and I'd still be lying there. One day she pulled back the covers and said, 'You've got to get up,' and I was there with my eyes shut tight going, 'I'm saying my prayers – give me five more minutes!'

KIMBERLEY: We were literally confined to the house

most of the time – it still wasn't public knowledge who'd made the final 10 – with the odd day out to do a photo shoot or something, but we were all there focused on this one thing so a lot of the time we were practising and just helping each other. I'm really close to my family and I was seeing someone at the time, so being away was hard, but I found it easy to get on with the other girls. I don't remember any rules in the house but I did feel quite isolated from the outside world. We all had our phones so we were able to call people, but we couldn't have friends or family down to stay or anything and we were busy rehearsing and stuff so we didn't have loads of free time. There were two chaperones in the house with us, Irene and Jane, and they were both lovely. Irene was this real Cockney character and she'd have to get us up in the mornings. I was quite good at getting out of bed but she used to try and bribe Nadine, who shared a room with me, by bringing in a cup of tea just to ease the pain of having to get up early. Nadine wouldn't want to get up and Irene would be saying, 'Don't shoot the messenger!'

I only found out when I got into the house that we were going to have to do these live performances every week on TV and I was thinking, oh my God, I hope I can hold it together. It was full-on and I had a week to catch up. I think I was so overwhelmed with joy that I'd got a second chance I felt a bit like I'd got nothing to lose. The first live show, when I sang 'Baby Can I Hold You', was probably my least nervous performance, but it just got harder as the weeks went on and there was more resting on it. That first week nobody knew what to expect or how they were going to feel once they got out there on stage. Obviously, I'd come into the house late and just felt grateful to even be in the first show, so I didn't have too many expectations. I wasn't thinking any further than that first week. I thought if I got through it would be a bonus because I felt I was the underdog, so I just wanted to do the best I could. I focused on what I had to do and concentrated on singing into the camera, rather than thinking about the millions of people watching, and I felt I did all right in the circumstances.

NICOLA: Oh my God, the first day in the house. It was absolutely beautiful, in St George's Hill in Surrey, just amazing, with a pool and everything. I came in two weeks late, four days before the first live show. I arrived evening time, went to bed, got up the next morning, and everyone was arguing. I was like this calm breeze that had blown into nine hurricanes. I think one of the girls had had an argument with somebody else and everyone was crying. It was like, 'You look at me like this,' and 'You said that last week!' The vocal coach was saying, 'You need to pull together – this is terrible,' and I was thinking, what is this? It was like a mad house.

I shared a room with Cheryl and Aimee, one of the other girls, and it was the first time I'd really been away from home. I had a boyfriend, Carl, at home, and all my friends, and it was a massive thing for me, but I loved it. When I look back I was a baby, just silly things I didn't know, like how to blow-dry my hair. But oh my God, the leash was off and it was great. I was singing every day and that was a dream come true. Every day was filled up with rehearsing, working with the vocal coaches, or just pottering around and going through our songs ourselves. I loved living with loads of other girls. We had such a laugh. I remember drinking too much one night and jumping into the pool with all my clothes on.

The first week I was given 'River Deep, Mountain High' to sing and I was really grateful because it showed off my range. The song was right and everything was fitting together. I remember before the first show one of the girls saying, 'We've been here two weeks and if one of us goes and *she* gets through after only just coming into the house, I'm gonna go off it.' Sure enough, she was the first person voted out.

SARAH: Girls can be bitchy and I'm just not interested in that whole catty vibe. It became very cliquey in the house and I'm not really a girls' girl. I've never had a sister, always been a bit of a tomboy, maybe not to look at, although more now I've got short hair. When I had long blonde hair and was a bit more tarted up people probably thought I was a bit of a bimbo, but I really wasn't. I was always the same person, just hiding behind a different mask.

The girls didn't get me at all at first. I was so bubbly and over the top they thought I was just putting on an act for the cameras. I am very flamboyant and outrageous but then the other side of me is the complete opposite. Even in the house I just felt they thought I was fake, which I'm not. I was crying every night, locking myself in my room because I just felt no one got me. I'm always very open and upfront and honest, and they know that now, but back then was a really hard time for me. I just felt like no one understood me. A lot of people think I'm either too in your face or a bit too moody when they first meet me. Over the years I've learned that if I don't smile I look moody, so I started becoming a bit more overly bubbly. I'd be the crazy one because if I wasn't, if I just sat being quiet, it looked like I had a strop on. I've just got one of those faces – I look like I'm hacked off when I'm not.

I don't know if anyone in the house realized how I felt. I'm quite guarded with people I don't know; it's part of a defence mechanism I've built up over the years. I was out of my comfort zone, put in a house with nine other girls, and I felt I was out of my depth. At some points I wondered if it was really worth it, but it taught me to be strong. If I've ever felt like giving up I just think, come on, you've been through the worst, don't throw it all away.

NADINE: The first week I sang 'Show Me Heaven' and the judges' comments were good. I didn't really have a sense of the girls competing with each other. You never tried to outshine anyone; it was a group effort, just trying to help people with their songs. We were heading for a group so it didn't feel like a competition to us. It only felt like that when we were actually in the band and battling with the boys.

SARAH: The live shows were awful. I can't say there was one performance on that programme when I sang my best. Nerves for me were the biggest thing and I still think I've got a lot to prove when it comes to my vocals, and maybe dancing, but I'm not so fussed about that. I was quite confident for the first show. I just wanted to get on the stage and do it and I actually opted to go first. Big mistake. Wrong song, wrong key. It was too low for me; it just didn't suit me. I sang 'Build Me Up Buttercup' and it's a really sentimental tune, which I thought would be a nice opener. I didn't really like the way I looked, the styling, but looking back I know what they were trying to do. They wanted to show that we were progressing, so the first week they wanted us to look as normal as we could, and week by week gradually turn us into the people who eventually got into the band.

CHERYL: The first show was the worst, just horrific. To get up and sing live, millions of people watching, having an opinion and judging you, knowing if you hit a bum note that's it, it was all a bit much. I was singing 'Baby Now That I've Found You' and my body was overtaken by nerves. All my family and friends were there, and when I heard my name in the run-up to going on I just wanted to die. I wanted to say, look, I'm not doing it. I can't. Every week, I'd be nervous all the way through until I'd finished the song. I had no control over my body: my legs were gone, my arms were gone, and I could hear it in my voice. One week I couldn't contain my nerves and the nurse gave me a herbal anti-hysteria tablet to put under my tongue, but it didn't kick in until after I'd sung.

I'd never felt like that before and I don't think I ever will again because we've experienced a lot now and I've realized if you make a mistake or hit a bad note, so what, big deal, whereas before my whole world would have crumbled. I'm older now and happier with myself and I know nobody's perfect, and that helps, definitely.

KIMBERLEY: I think me and Cheryl were probably the most nervous of the 10 girls. When you've grown up singing for people who just want to see you do well it's hard to explain what a different feeling it is singing in front of people who are judging every single thing you do. It wasn't even so much the TV cameras and the millions of people watching, because I used to block that out and concentrate on the studio audience, it was the judgement thing. I couldn't help feeling nervous and worried the judges were going to pull me to shreds. The first week wasn't so bad because there was an element of excitement, but every other week I'd be nervous, trying to focus myself and not spread panic. The second week I sang 'Unbreak My Heart'. I'd been getting quite a lot of support and encouragement from the vocal coaches in rehearsals so I felt good about my voice and the song, but I felt there was more resting on that performance. I knew somebody had to go and I didn't want it to be me. I remember the trousers I was wearing were awful; they'd taken them up too much and they were at half-mast, so I didn't feel comfortable about how I looked. Literally, between the dress run and the live show they whipped them off me and tried to let the hems down a bit. I was okay with my performance and I got quite good comments from the judges but when the votes came in I was in the bottom two with Chloe. I was standing there with her and Davina waiting to find out if I was leaving and it's weird because I remember thinking it was fine, that I could deal with it, and looking for my family in the audience to let them know I was all right. I didn't want them getting upset. I just felt I wasn't going to collapse in a heap on the floor if Davina said my name. When Chloe went she didn't take it very well. It's fine to be upset but she was really unhappy about it. She really thought it should have been her that stayed. I was glad to stay and in a way feeling the public preferred me to be there gave me a little spurt of confidence.

CHERYL: Every week it got harder. I remember being happy I'd got through the first show but at the same time thinking to myself, I can't blag it. I've always been realistic about my vocal ability. I chose to sing 'You're Still The One' in week two. It was my dad and his wife's wedding song, and also my nana had passed away a year before and it was her favourite song, so I was kind of hoping if I sang to her she'd be watching over me and would help me through, and it seemed to work. I was quite comfortable singing it because it wasn't a Mariah song or a Whitney song, which would have been a massive challenge. I think that was my most comfortable week because I knew what I was in for. My family and friends were there again, I don't think I'd had great comments from the judges in the first week, and I just knew I had to go for it.

NICOLA: There were people being sick, crying, taking herbal pills to calm them down, so nervous about the live shows, and I'd be like, bring it on. It was my dream come true, totally. I was in my

element, so appreciative to be singing live for millions of viewers every week. It was so my thing. The second week I sang 'Shout' and I think because I hadn't been in the bottom two girls in week one I felt safe, like I wasn't clinging on to be there. I remember Kimberley was like, 'I can't do it,' and I'd be saying – 'Pull yourself together!' I absolutely loved it. The rest of the girls hated it but I loved the fact I was singing all the time and getting recognition for it.

SARAH: I lost my confidence as the weeks went by. The second week Louis wanted me to sing 'Anyone Who Had a Heart', and apparently that was one of the best performances I did, but I didn't know the song and I thought it was too old-fashioned for me, and the styling was horrendous. That show was probably my least favourite. I just hated my hair and make-up and I had this long velvety dress on. I looked like I'd aged about 20 years.

NADINE: The second week I sang 'Fields of Gold', which was my audition song. I just tried to think about what I was singing, not about whether I'd get into the band or not. I wanted to sing to the best of my ability and feel happy with my performance, so all week I practised really hard, over and over, from first thing in the morning until last thing at night, just making sure I felt comfortable and confident with the song. That's what it was about to me. I didn't really think about the judges' comments or people voting until the song was over, then it was, okay, I could get kicked out now, but it was more about doing a good job and being able to feel proud and happy.

KIMBERLEY: The third week I was singing 'Emotions', the Bee Gees song, although I was more familiar with the Destiny's Child version, and I just freaked out, similar to how I had in the auditions. Maybe subconsciously I was thinking it was my week to go. The song is usually split into parts for different people to sing and I underestimated how hard it was going to be to sing it on my own and breathe with my nerves the way they were. Me and Nadine were sharing a room and were really close from the beginning and the thought that one of us might go was freaking both of us out. She ended up having a panic attack. I think in hindsight she was more scared I would go and there was nothing she could do about it. I didn't feel confident about my performance, I just felt I could have done better, which was frustrating, and I was trying to hold back the tears. Davina was trying to talk to me and I couldn't speak because I knew I'd burst out crying. That night I got through but afterwards I still couldn't speak. I didn't even know why I felt like that. I do consider myself quite laid-back and quite tough – I can normally take most things in my stride – but when you care about something that much it brings out emotions you don't even know you have. I'd done *Les Mis* as a child, when I was 11 or 12, and had to sing in front of 5,000 people, which should have been petrifying, but wasn't. I'd get nervous and excited, the usual feelings, but then I'd get the first word out and I'd be fine. But this wasn't like that at all. It was just an awful feeling.

NADINE: Every week I thought I wasn't going to make it. We had four live shows and my parents and whole family were flying over from Ireland to be there. They could have got cheaper flights if they'd booked them in advance, but there was always the thought I might get thrown out so they'd just make arrangements one week at a time. In week three I sang 'When I Fall In Love' and I was really nervous. That was my lowest point, my 'freak-out' moment. I was in the dressing room and Louis said, 'Oh, I think Kimberley's going tonight.' Me and Kimberley were really close and I just felt sick. I couldn't bear the thought of it. The nurse gave me a herbal tablet to put under my tongue to calm my nerves and said by the time I went on stage it would have dissolved, but there was no saliva in my mouth and it wasn't going anywhere. Some of the other girls were going through the same thing. I was just afraid, panic-stricken, and I was up first that week. I don't know how I managed to sing. I used to try and

> ❛ I told Louis he'd ruined the entire show for me, that I was panicking the whole time that Kimberley would go . . . ❜

sing in all types of situations and it came out every time so how I rationalized it in my mind was, why would it not come out this time? I told myself it'd be fine, don't think about it, your voice will take over when you start to sing, you'll go into autopilot. I don't remember the judges' comments at all. As soon as the song was over my mind switched off. Afterwards, I told Louis he'd ruined the entire show for me, that I was panicking the whole time that Kimberley would go, and did he feel bad. But he doesn't think about the sensitivities of girls worrying about their friends.

CHERYL: People think reality TV is easy, but it's not. A lot of artists are groomed and styled and given media training and singing lessons before they're put out there but we were raw, singing on live TV every week and being judged and that makes it harder, if anything. Because of my previous relationship and massive insecurities the thought of being judged was a big deal for me. I've always been hard on myself anyway, my own worst critic, and I found the process hard to bear.

I shared a room in the house with Aimee and then when Nicola arrived she came in with us. Aimee was my little pal and I took care of her. She was younger, really sweet, and then there was the show in week three where it was between me and her who'd go. I'd sung 'Nothing Compares To You' and at that point I was prepared to go home if it meant she could stay. That was the closest result in the whole series, with 1,218 votes between us. When she went I felt terrible, then afterwards someone from the show said they were sorry to have had to do that to us but it made great TV. That was the start of me realizing this industry is ruthless, cut-throat. I'd made it through to the next round and I should have been happy but I wasn't. It was horrible.

KIMBERLEY: I was in the bottom three with Cheryl and Aimee in week three and when it came down to the two of them it was just awful. All of us loved both of them and it was getting to the point we were all so close that we didn't want anybody to go. I certainly didn't want either of them to leave. Aimee was the baby of the group and it was hard watching her go through that horrible experience of waiting to find out if she was leaving. You could see it was absolutely killing her, almost too much for her to take. That affected all of us because everybody was so sad after that and it took a good few days to get any sense of happiness back in the house.

NADINE: You're under the glare of the judges, the production company people, all trying to make a show, and you don't know any better so you treat them all like teachers. They tell you what to do and being so young you feel inferior and then it's flipped around and you're thinking of a career and making really important decisions, so it's strange. I'd done Irish *Popstars*, which had aired six months before. It got me used to having cameras around and being judged, as much as you can get used to it, but it was all a bit of a blur *Popstars: The Rivals* was a much bigger deal – a UK record label and millions of viewers. It just seemed more real, on a bigger scale.

When I went for the Irish *Popstars* audition I was 16 and you were supposed to be 18. I was signing in and they said to write down my date of birth, then when I put 15 June 1985, someone said, 'Change that five to a three and you'll be grand.' Then, before you knew it, I was in the band. I told loads of people at the time how old I was but nobody was saying anything. Once I was in the band it was like, we have to say something now. Getting kicked out for being too young wasn't what bothered me, because I never expected to be in the band in the first place, what really bothered me was that they let it happen the way they did. People must have known before I got into the band that I was under age. When it happened it just made me feel there's nothing real about reality TV. Nobody's natural when there's a camera around and some of the stuff I can't even watch it's so scripted and false and fake and fickle.

SARAH: The third week I put my foot down and said I wanted to sing 'I'll Be There', which is what I used to sing on the circuit a lot when I was doing gigs and things, but they made me put it down a key and I don't like singing things too low. I did my own hair and make-up that week. I suppose looking back I probably did look a bit slutty! But it was the one week I felt most comfortable and at ease with myself.

NICOLA: I sang 'Wind Beneath My Wings' in week three. I was thinking the numbers were getting smaller now and it was a really big deal. Every week before I went on stage I used to go to the toilet, to the same cubicle, and pray, just ask God to please let me have this. Even though I was confident in my singing ability, and I knew I had a stronger voice than most, at the same time I still had a little bit of insecurity because I'd been told Louis didn't want me. I was never in the bottom two, though, and the producers told me I always came in the top two or three in terms of votes each week, which was great.

CHERYL: The night the band was named I sang 'Right Here Waiting'. The seats were set out for the five and when we were rehearsing during the day I looked at the first seat and something inside was telling me that was mine. I just had a really strong feeling. Then on the night when Davina was about to announce the first band member I could hear her saying my name before she actually did and I think that's why I reacted the way I did and jumped in the air and shouted, 'Come on!', because that was my chair. I was in the band.

That night when I got to the hotel I just lay in the room looking up at the ceiling in disbelief. The only word I can use to describe the feeling was euphoric. It was amazing, almost like a buzz going through my body. I couldn't believe I'd done it. I didn't have pushy parents, no one saying I would do it. I just felt I'd achieved it myself and it was a dream come true. People had picked up the phone and voted for me and that was enough. I don't think I slept that night, I was just in a trance, then in the morning I texted all the girls saying, 'We're in the band. We ARE the band!'.

NICOLA: The night we got into the band I'd performed 'I'm So Excited'. I was feeling nervous because they made this big thing on the programme about people not voting the way they had been in previous weeks. They were saying the girls that everyone might think were safe weren't necessarily getting the votes, so I was like, what the hell's going on? When we were waiting for Davina to reveal the band I remember being so petrified. When she started to say the first name I didn't feel it would be me. She called out Cheryl's name and I just thought, thank God. She'd been in the bottom two the week before and that was awful, so I was so glad she was first in the band. Then Davina started to say who the second member of the band was and I just knew she was going to say my name. It was so weird, it totally freaked me out. I remember looking at my mum and dad in the audience when I went to take my seat next to Cheryl and they were jumping up and down and I felt so proud for them. I thought, 'I'm in the band!' It was an unbelievable feeling.

NADINE: On the last show I sang 'I Wanna Dance With Somebody'. I'd been taking things day by day, not thinking about the end result, even when it got to the point where Davina was calling out the five band members, and then it suddenly hit me. Oh my God! I started crying as she said the names … Cheryl, Nicola, me, Kimberley, and then Sarah. I was in tears as I went to take my seat and I just sat there crying.

KIMBERLEY: The night the band was revealed I sang 'Chain Reaction'. I was so drained by the whole process by then and finally I was going to know one way or another and I was just grateful for that. I thought, at least whatever happens I can get on with my life and not have to do this ever again, because it was a horrible experience in a lot of ways. I thought I'd just try and enjoy myself that night and see what happened, if it was meant to be. There was an element of relief, pure elation that I was in, but then there was also the realization that it was going to affect my life and my friends and my boyfriend.

SARAH: I'm a very emotional person; I go at things like a bull in a china shop, and until you get to know me you won't see the sensitive side. I'm an emotional wreck sometimes. I'd rather people see me being kooky and a bit lairy than upset – that's a sign of weakness in my eyes – but they love a bit of drama on TV. I was constantly in tears but I also came across as bubbly and lively. Because I'm a performer, I'm good at switching things on when I have to, but it was probably the worst emotional rollercoaster I have ever been on, the most nerve-racking, pressurized situation I've ever been in. Looking back, though, I know it's made me stronger; that it was character-building and made me a tougher person. I suppose in a way it helped prepare me for what was to come.

The night I got in the band was probably the worst and the best in my life. One of the boys had suggested I sing 'Holding Out For a Hero', and I nearly lost my voice before the show because I'd been pushing it and pushing it, wanting to do key changes and just the best performance ever. I was a little bit off-key on some bits, really struggling because I'd lost my voice through all the rehearsals the week before, and I was just so nervous. I think the nerves made me ten times worse, but it was still a wicked performance.

I didn't feel the public wanted me because I was the last one in and then there was the whole scandal over the voting and people saying it was rigged, that it should have been Javine [Hylton]. There were viewers who said they'd voted for Javine

and got a text back to say they'd voted for me and was it a fix? I just felt, why is this happening? I didn't feel I was accepted into the band for a while because I didn't feel I was the one that should have been there.

NICOLA: We had our photos done, had a bit of a party, then Louis introduced us to John [McMahon], our tour manager. We were like, 'What's your job?' We were so naïve. John was in it with us. He worked as hard as we did the two weeks we were on the road, battling the boys. He drove us everywhere, organized

everything, and just took care of us. I remember we were always freezing in the car and wanted the heating on and poor John in the front seat had hot air blowing directly on him all the time. After two weeks on the road he had terrible dry skin and chapped lips.

KIMBERLEY: Once we were in the band, what began was another phase of weirdness. The first two weeks it was a whirlwind, working every possible hour leading up to Christmas. I've worked hard, but never that hard. It was literally three hours' sleep every night and you got through it on adrenalin because you were doing what you'd dreamed of all your life. You just do it and don't really think of it as hard work, but when I look back it was full-on; just the lifestyle and working out what it means to be in a band and be a pop star. None of us knew anything; we weren't aware of the whole promotions cycle and what you have to do. Now it's all normal to us, but back then we just didn't know.

It was an amazing time, though, because we were swept into this world where we were taken care of and had people doing our hair and make-up – things we just weren't used to. Straight away we were doing shows like *Top of the Pops*, which we'd grown up watching every week, and suddenly we were there and it was just the pinnacle. The first time we did *CD:UK* Mariah Carey, Westlife, and Justin Timberlake were on and we were just young girls, completely star-struck. I'd grown up admiring those people and to be in the same realm as them was just the maddest thing ever. We loved every second of it.

NICOLA: I don't remember much about making the video for 'Sound of the Underground'. We got in the band on the Saturday night and on the Monday morning we were in this old, derelict warehouse doing the video. It was freezing cold and I remember hearing the song playing on the radio and someone asking how I wanted my hair and I was like, I don't know – straight? I hadn't a clue. Then we got dressed and did it.

We have never worked so hard as when we were promoting the single. We would go to every single radio station, get home at two in the morning, and be up again at four for *GMTV*. That's what it was like for two weeks running.

At one point I was having my make-up done, I think it was at *GMTV*, and I'd fallen asleep, completely passed out, and the make-up artist was slapping my face and going, 'Nicola? Nicola?' He couldn't wake me, that's how tired we were. John, our tour manager, came running in and was shaking me. He was the only person we had really, he was like our dad, and we completely relied on him. He was such a lovely man. We were just five young girls and we didn't know anything. All I'd ever had to do was get up for school. He used to say things like, 'The record company want us to do one more TV and it means getting three hours' sleep instead of six …' and we'd be saying, 'We can't, we physically can't work any more.' He'd be going, 'Come on, girls, we can do this, we can get this number one.' He was like the sixth member, having as little sleep as we were, and we felt like we were all in it together.

SARAH: When we made the video for 'Sound of the Underground' I'd had about four hours' sleep and I was sitting in the Winnebago and every news channel was running the story about us and the voting 'scandal'. I was in tears thinking, I'm just not meant to be here and I'm so sick of crying.

That's probably why I've become a lot more bolshy and give the attitude that I don't care, even though I do. I just had to pull my socks up, get on with it and show everyone I do deserve to be in the band. Now I just go fingers up to them all. It was mental to start with – TV, photo shoots, a radio tour, up at the crack of dawn every morning, not back until late. The tiredness was horrific. I can't cope at the best of times. I'm good under certain pressure but not that tired pressure – I just crumble – so I don't know what got me through all that. Maybe it was nervous energy and excitement and wanting to prove I was good enough.

KIMBERLEY: We'd been led to believe the boys would do better than us and we just thought it wasn't the end of the world even if we didn't get to number one. We knew we had a good song and we knew we had a good video. We were so happy when we saw the video because we didn't have a clue what we were doing, but we felt we had blagged it quite well. We just tried to help each other, and bearing in mind it was done a couple of days after getting into the band, I think we did a pretty good job. The video was a bit more edgy than the boys' one. We saw it together on a big screen at ITV and we were all screaming, just so proud we'd managed to pull it off.

NADINE: We were definitely the underdogs and that's how we felt. You just think girls buy into boy bands and it's rare that a girl band crosses over and appeals to everybody, so we were just working really hard. We thought we weren't going to get to number one, that it would be One True Voice, but we had a song we were proud of, and if it was in the charts, that was great.

We were working really hard and we lived in this really strange place. It was like flats/hotel rooms in Westminster. It was almost like a retirement home. We were terrified of it. What scared us was the night we moved in Cheryl and Nicola ran into a guy in his underpants who'd come out to complain about the noise. We were coming in at all hours in the night and leaving at all hours in the morning. We'd have a shower, lie down for a couple of hours, get up, throw some clothes on and go again. We were afraid of who we'd meet in the lift, which sounds crazy now, but we were afraid of our own shadows. John had to go and buy us socks and underwear we were so busy. I don't think anything had sunk in then.

NICOLA: To start with, we were living out of plastic bags. We would stroll up to these five-star hotels, our hair all over, no sleep, trackies and trainers on, and our clothes in carrier bags. John was like, 'Girls, I'm so embarrassed to walk into hotels with you. I've bought you a present.' He actually bought five little suitcases for us. We didn't understand that hotels could do our laundry, so instead of washing our clothes we'd buy new ones, then we'd have more suitcases full of dirty washing. It was ridiculous.

SARAH: There were rumours going round that Girls Aloud were impossible to work with – divas – and I don't doubt some of it was true because we were tired all the time. We were working so hard – constantly doing radio interviews and press and TV – and we were snappy at times, but it wasn't personal. At the end

of the day no one taught us how to be professional, we didn't have any media training or anything. We were learning, but I think in the end what worked for us was being real. I loved 'Sound of the Underground' because people were expecting a typical girly band sound and it was so different.

CHERYL: For two weeks we worked so hard because we had to battle against the boys for the Christmas number one. It was 24/7, the hardest we've worked I think, and there was nothing glamorous about it. We'd jump in the car to go to Birmingham, Newcastle, Glasgow, Aberdeen and back to London ... we didn't know where we were in the end. We were getting pizzas and stopping at McDonald's all the time. We put on a lot of weight and the media noticed so the scrutiny started. We had to push ourselves because everyone was backing the boys and we were the underdogs. We knew we had to step up our game, push ourselves to do another performance even if we hadn't slept, and it gave us motivation. A motto of mine is 'make the haters your motivators' and we really did. We wanted to prove we could do it.

KIMBERLEY: I think as a group straight away we just looked and gelled better than the boys. They had two that were quite small, one really tall, and unfortunately it does matter. We had a really good mix of elements that worked. I think ultimately the reason we beat them, though, was the song. The boys did a typical pop formula and the public just didn't buy into it. They wanted something fresh and 'Sound of the Underground' was a really cutting record.

I also think what the record company did with the marketing campaign was very clever. We had Peter Loraine and Poppy Stanton and a fantastic team at Polydor handling our campaign and they came up with this 'BUY GIRLS – BYE BOYS' slogan. Thinking back, that was just another of their moments of genius. Our single was on two different formats as well – one had a different mix and interviews – and lots of people bought both. Our marketing guys also persuaded Davina to do a 'Buy Girls' ad and ran it on Capital Radio when the boys were in doing an interview, which was really cheeky but very effective. We had posters all over London and on our car and it definitely helped.

When we got to number one we were euphoric. It was a dream come true. We'd all been trying so hard for so long to make it we just felt on top of the world.

SARAH: No offence, but the boys came out with some serious rubbish with 'Sacred Trust'. I have respect for a few of the boys in One True Voice. Daniel Pearce was an amazing singer and

Anton Gordon was really talented – but they did have the wrong song. It was amazing getting to number one, and staying there for four weeks was a huge achievement, but it was like I didn't really appreciate it at the time because it didn't feel real. It was all so new to us. I had to keep pinching myself because I couldn't quite believe it was really happening. I thought I was going to wake up and it would all be a dream. We were in a bubble and we hadn't had the chance to adapt to things. Looking back, I feel so proud of what we achieved but at the time we were working so hard we didn't really get time to let our hair down and celebrate.

NICOLA: Halfway through the week before we found out who'd got the number one we were all in the car and our song came on the radio, then the boys' song came on, and I just had this feeling that if we beat them we were going to be fine, that everything would be okay, and we'd be on this journey together for a long time.

NADINE: The night we got to number one, it was announced on TV but we knew beforehand and the boys knew too. I felt bad because our dressing rooms were attached and we were screaming and jumping round the canteen at LWT and the poor boys were in the next room. They came in with a bottle of champagne and said well done. I think we got there because 'Sound of the Underground' was something new and different. I still love that song.

It was so exciting, really amazing to have done so well; that was what we'd worked for. After all the effort we'd put into the shows and recording the song, to know that people in the UK really liked it and had responded to it was a great feeling. It felt like all those mornings we'd been getting up at four o'clock, all that being ill, waking up and wanting to throw up just from tiredness – it was all worthwhile because people had bought the single. There was something really magical and special about that time, and it's funny but certain smells always remind me of it – like there was a Body

Shop coconut body lotion I always wore then and every time I put that on it takes me right back there.

CHERYL: During the race for the number one we didn't have a clue. The boys were 60,000 copies behind us on the first day, or something, and we thought they still might catch up. We didn't know we were so far ahead – it was impossible. I think we beat the boys because we had a great song, something unusual; there was nothing like it out there at the time. 'Sound of the Underground' was a really good pop track. The boys had a rubbish song. They were all incredibly talented individually but they just didn't gel as a band, whereas we clicked straight away, thankfully. We were like a force. I think people bought into our song and there was a niche in the market for a girl band and we stole it.

To be Christmas number one was a special feeling. When I was growing up my dad was always the one telling me to get my head out of the clouds. I'd always said to him, 'When I'm Christmas number one on *Top of the Pops* I'll prove you wrong …' They did this homecoming thing for me in a local pub after I got in the band and my dad did a speech and said, 'In fairness, she told me she'd be on *Top of the Pops* with the Christmas number one and now I'm eating a big slice of humble pie.' That was an amazing feeling.

being **GIRLS**

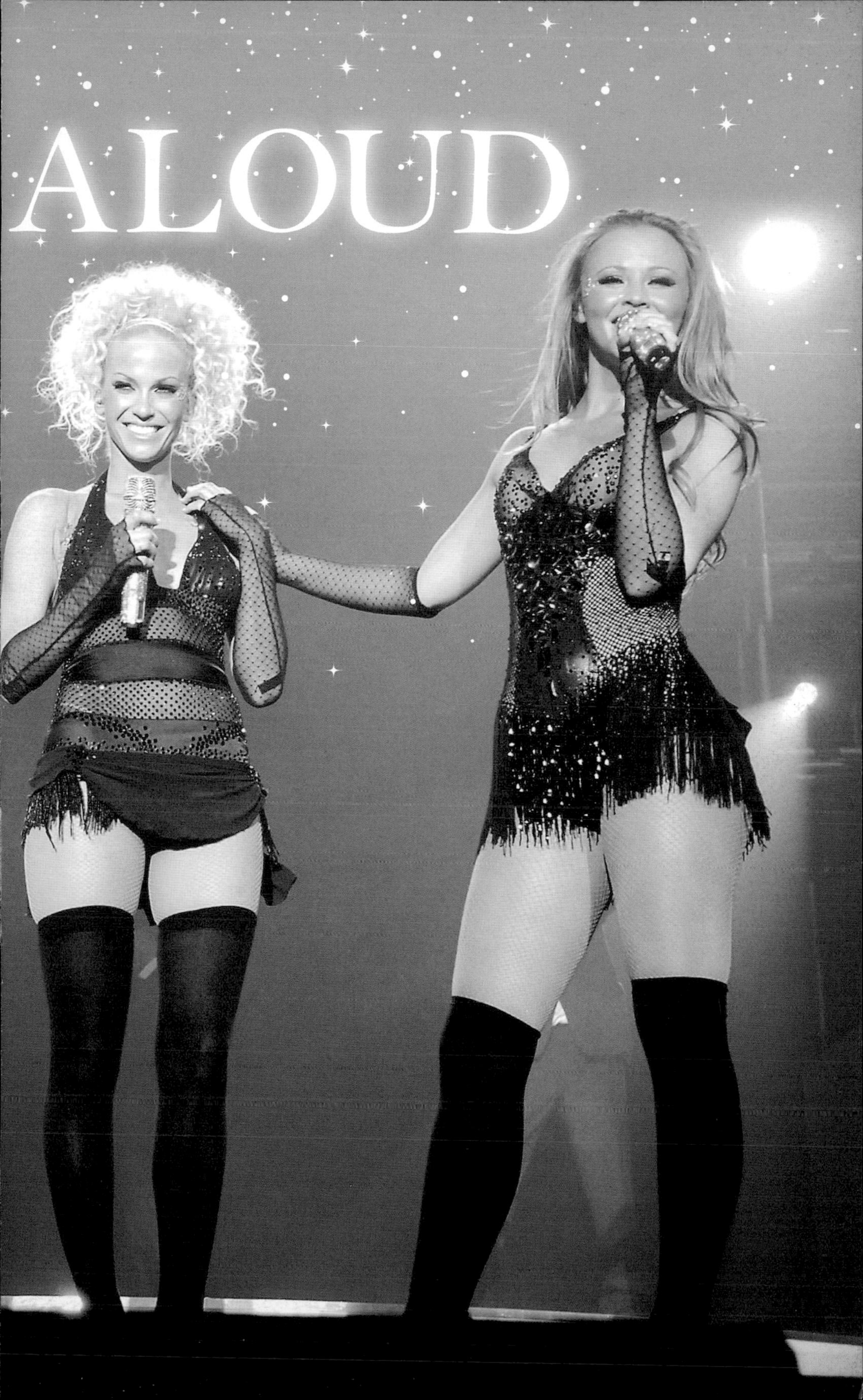
ALOUD

Christmas 2002. With 'Sound of the Underground' at number one and the girls riding high there's tragic news when tour manager John McMahon dies in a car crash on Christmas Day. In January 2003, Cheryl faces assault charges after an incident in a nightclub. Meanwhile, the single tops the charts for four weeks and, with sales of 550,000, goes gold. The girls start work on their début album. The second single, 'No Good Advice', charts at number two in May 2003. Behind the scenes the girls contend with domestic disasters and relationship break-ups.

NADINE: It hadn't really sunk in that I was in this band and what that meant. I still have points now where it doesn't seem real. Even when we were back home and the single was number one it didn't make sense. You don't know how you're supposed to feel so you don't feel anything. You don't really know what's going on. You're like, right, okay, we're number one ... then you just throw yourself into the next thing. The first week in the band there was a story saying I was leaving. We'd worked all those weeks and months to get there, 'Sound of the Underground' was at number one, and the first week it was, 'Nadine's leaving, she's going solo.' They love to think that. It's a lot more exciting than 'Girls Aloud discuss everything together as a group.' I just thought it was hilarious, that it made no sense whatsoever. Why would I go? Where did that come from? Where do any of the rumours come from? I'm always supposed to be leaving the band; the fans don't like to read it but I've no control over it. There's nothing I can do – maybe stand on London Bridge and shout 'I am not leaving!', but I'd have to do it every other day.

❛ I'm always supposed to be leaving the band . . . There's nothing I can do – maybe stand on London Bridge and shout "I am not leaving!" every other day. ❜

We were really lonely when we came back after Christmas to record the album. We'd lost John, our tour manager. Louis had phoned me on Christmas Day to tell me he'd passed away and I couldn't get my head round it. I was just shocked – what? Our John? I phoned the girls and told them but it didn't become real until it was in the newspaper and it was our car and our things lying in the grass at the side of the road. It was awful, just awful.

He'd worked as hard as we had and he was so happy and excited – it was 'WE are number one.' We went to the funeral and he had a family, young kids. You feel bad because his life was taken away so abruptly and for what? His family had lost their father. I couldn't imagine that happening to me, what I'd do, yet when there's a death people seem to get the strength from somewhere to tell everybody else it's okay. We dedicated 'Stay Another Day', the B-side of 'Sound of the Underground', to him.

NICOLA: I remember going home for Christmas and New Year and 'Sound of the Underground' was at number one. On Christmas Day I got a text from John McMahon and you know how it is when you're getting loads of texts and you're having your dinner or something so you think, I'll catch you later. Then the next day I got a call to say he'd been in a crash and died, and that was just horrible. I remember after I'd got the call I just stayed in my bedroom and cried. I was supposed to be going to my auntie's house for more Christmas celebrations but I didn't move until the next day. I don't think I stopped crying all night. It was a mixture of guilt because I hadn't texted back and because he'd spent all his time with us and not his own children; it was also a big release of all the emotions of the last couple of months.

KIMBERLEY: On Christmas Day I'd sat with my family watching us on *Top of the Pops* thinking someone pinch me, this is mad, then on Boxing Day I got a call from Nadine about John and it just knocked me for six. It was hard because we'd all been so busy in that two-week period leading up to Christmas, so tired and on edge, I didn't even feel we'd seen the best of each other and that made it hard to accept he was gone. We'd got really close to him in a short period of time and it just felt surreal. The plan had been for him to work with us long-term. As far as we were concerned he was brilliant, great at the job – which isn't easy with five girls. The tour manager is like the sixth member of the band, he's with you just about 24 hours a day, so you need someone everybody's happy with – and that was John. I think we were a bit spoiled with him because he knew how to deal with us, he had a different relationship with each girl, and it wasn't easy finding someone else.

SARAH: I was in the Trafford Centre in Manchester on Boxing Day with one of my ex-boyfriends when I got a call from Poppy [Stanton] at the record company. She said, 'John's died,' and it took me a moment to register. I just broke down. That really tore us up. We were on such a high having him as our mentor in the beginning, there with us every second through that hard transition period, and for him to be gone, we did feel a little bit lost. It was really devastating and we didn't have long to grieve for him because we were straight into the studio and recording. We didn't really get time to get over it.

CHERYL: Because everything was new, everyone around us was special. On Boxing Day Poppy from the record company phoned and said she had some really tragic news. I thought something had happened to one of the girls, but it was that John had died in a car accident. It was like, what is going on? That was a horrible feeling. He was like the sixth member of the band at the time. We all went to the funeral and that was quite a bonding process, I suppose, to go through that with four other girls because we only had each other.

NICOLA: It wasn't until after I got in the band that it started to hit home that I was a different person now and it was weird and difficult to deal with. Until then, I'd been focused on having this chance and wanting to take it, just striving to achieve my goal.

At that point my mum and dad were breaking up. My little sister, Frankie, was 13 and she was in turmoil; her head was absolutely messed up. I had two little brothers, Harrison, who was five, and Clayton, who was two, so I was still very much part of a young family, but suddenly I was also in this band.

Things had changed and the first time I really knew that was on New Year's Eve when I went out with my friends and my boyfriend. My dad didn't want me to go out but I just wanted to be a teenager. I didn't want to be restricted. What was I supposed to do on New Year's Eve – sit in? I said, 'I won't drink, I'll be sensible.' We went to this little dive of a nightclub, horrible place. I'd been there six weeks before, just a normal person, but now everybody was looking at me. People I went to school with were different with me, all saying things like, 'I bet you've got loads of money now, blah blah blah.' I just wanted to dance with everyone like I always did and fit in with my normal friends, do everything I used to, but on the other hand I was a pop star and it was just weird. My drink was spiked that night. I knew it had been because I'd been really responsible and only had two drinks all night but when I got home I got ill and started spewing up, and all the next day I felt really bad.

NADINE: I remember coming back in the New Year to do the album, stuck in the middle of nowhere by ourselves, no John, just sitting round the dinner table one night crying. It seems we did a lot of crying in the beginning. We didn't even have anywhere to do our washing or dry anything and we were just getting by, buying new things. We brought our washing to Brian Higgins from Xenomania, who writes and produces our albums. Our clothes were all over his house, drying on the radiators.

NICOLA: We were recording the album and staying in this hotel in Surrey that had five bedrooms – a crookedy haunted little thing in the middle of nowhere. I just felt I needed to go out but we were already famous and had everybody talking about us. There was a sense of being lonely and trapped. Even with the rest of the girls, as close as we were and as much as we got on it wasn't like we'd known each other for years. It was like we were growing up in front of the country, everybody criticizing us for going out and having a few drinks like normal girls, people saying, 'These are terrible role models, blah blah blah.' Hang on a minute – I'm 17 years old and I feel lost. I need a role model myself.

> ❛ It was like we were growing up in front of the country, everybody criticizing us for going out and having a few drinks like normal girls, people saying, 'These are terrible role models, blah blah blah.' Hang on a minute – I'm 17 years old . . . I need a role model myself. ❜

SARAH: Our first album was a real mix of producers. We were trying to find who gelled with us best and it was Brian Higgins, so we've worked more or less constantly with him. It's been tough at times because I didn't always see eye to eye with him in the beginning. He's very good at what he does and at the same time he's a bit eccentric, a genius, and with me being very outspoken and quite opinionated we didn't get off to the best start. I think it took him a while to warm to a couple of us, but down the line he now seems to have immense respect for us and we feel we're his muses. He can be very blunt, but I think we appreciate his honesty because it's all constructive criticism and it makes us work harder. His songwriting partner, Miranda [Cooper], is great as well. They earwig us and work off our energy. On the first album you could really tell which weren't Brian's songs, which songs worked for us and which didn't, and where we felt the formula was working we stuck to it. He can be very diverse and change the style of the music but still have our quirky lyrics and tongue-in-cheek attitude. He manages to get the same vibe running through what we do without it getting boring. He's been a godsend to us.

KIMBERLEY: It took a while to gel with Brian [Higgins] because he's such a genius; it can be a bit scary when you first meet him, a bit intimidating. We all had immediate respect for him because he'd produced 'Sound of the Underground' and I think when we were doing the album, although we worked with different producers, we had the most faith in him. We didn't actually think the album was that good when we first heard it, so we went to him and said his songs were great but we needed more

of that calibre. He must have had some belief in us because he went to the record company and said he'd do six more songs so we could pick the ones we wanted for the album. We ended up replacing some of the original tracks and it just rounded the album off.

NICOLA: Brian had done 'Sound of the Underground' and come up with this quirky sound. We worked with a few other people on the first album but Brian was the one coming up with the goods. Everything his songs brought – the electro parts, the rhythms that weren't mainstream – became our sound. We were very young, very outspoken, very naïve, quite ballsy, but a bit lost at the same time, and I think he took his inspiration from that. As a collective we had this aura, this personality, and I don't think he'd come across five girls like that before. We're definitely girls who won't settle for second best, we constantly want to improve, and we were impressed by Brian and the sounds he was coming out with, and proud of the fact our songs were so different to anybody else's.

NADINE: We were in the position of releasing our first single and having a huge hit before we worked on the album, so by the time we started every producer had heard 'Sound of the Underground' and everything they were doing was just a bad imitation of that. Everything sounded like the single, only not as good, and we just thought if everyone's trying to copy Brian anyway, why don't we just work with him? So that's what we did. He was the one setting the trend and he's always been very music forward; thinking about what's next rather than what's happening right now.

CHERYL: I like the fact we've only ever worked with Brian. It's unique in pop really to work with the same producer, but we've got a formula, so why change it? We did do a few songs on the first album with other producers that weren't up to his standard at all. He eats, sleeps, breathes and dreams music. His life revolves around music. There's definitely something, a chemistry between him and us, that works.

NICOLA: We'd all grown up watching *CD:UK* every Saturday morning and it was totally our thing. Then we got in the band and we were there almost every week and we were so excited about it. Seeing the other side, the gritty side, getting to perform, was just amazing. It was what we'd all dreamed of. We were on with people like Mary J. Blige and Justin Timberlake but we didn't need the big names to make it feel like, wow. It was already a massive deal to us. I remember performing 'No Good Advice', our second single, in 2003, and forgetting to mime my line. We just weren't with it. Then, I think a week later, we were on again. We had this New York taxi in the studio and our choreographer had planned a big performance. We had dancers for the first time so there was that whole boy/girl chemistry thing and it was just so awkward having to dance with these boys and jump off the taxi and try to be sexy. If I look back at that now I can't relate to who we were then. It's like, who are those girls? It's so weird.

Doing shows like *CD:UK* and *Top of the Pops* was huge for us and we all appreciated what that meant, but at the same time we knew we had to make it feel normal or we'd lose our heads. Sometimes in the beginning I'd text my little sister to say we were at *Top of the Pops* and she'd be like, 'Oh my God!' But for us, doing those shows was our day-to-day routine. If you see it how you used to see it – 'I'm SO excited to be here!' – you're just going to look like an absolute divvy, so you have to make it normal, even though inside you know you're doing what you've always dreamed of and it's amazing.

KIMBERLEY: We spent half our lives at *CD:UK* and *SM:TV* in the early days. We were literally there almost every week. The studio, in the LWT building on the South Bank, which was where we'd done *Popstars: The Rivals*, just became such a familiar place to us. There were lots of bands around at that time, like Westlife, Blue and Atomic Kitten, and it was just really enjoyable. It was weird that we'd actually become part of a world we'd all been watching on television for so long.

NICOLA: I started to feel really guilty because I wasn't living in a little town any more with a job I didn't like. I had goals in my life and prospects. It was like somebody had opened a gate for me but not for my family, that's how it felt, and I'd started to have a bit of money to spend on myself whereas they were still in the same position. My dad was in the same job, working at Ford's, and my sister was getting a bit of stick at school, and I just felt guilty about it. It was hard to deal with.

At the same time, I wasn't this bubbly character like the other girls so I automatically stuck out. I had puppy fat, I was getting stick from people for the way I looked and the fact everyone thought I was miserable. I was lost, just lost. I couldn't adapt quick enough. I started thinking really deeply about life. I'd be like, why is this happening to me? I hated being pale, hated the way I looked, hated photo shoots and interviews because I was too shy and could never say the right thing. I hated a lot of things. I constantly felt like I wasn't up to scratch. I couldn't speak to people properly because I felt like people didn't want to speak to me. There were journalists saying I was the most pointless member of the band and it made me embarrassed about myself.

It was just a really weird, horrible time, and me and Cheryl – she had a bit of stuff going on then as well – we'd sit there and go, why?

CHERYL: It's never been an easy ride for Girls Aloud. I don't think people get that at all. It was a big struggle in the beginning to prove ourselves as a band and maintain the level of quality pop songs. Everybody was waiting to hear the album, waiting to see what we were going to do next, then there was the added pressure of bad press and people saying untrue things, especially when you're new to it. Now I read a story and I just think, whatever, but then it would break me down to the point I was like, is this really worth it?

In January 2003, I had only been in the band three or four weeks when there was the whole nightclub incident, and I went from being euphoric, having the time of my life, and thinking, oh my God, I can't believe my life, to feeling like it doesn't get any worse. Me and Nicola had gone to a club in Guildford, in great spirits, the single was at number one. They were happy for us to be there and sent over champagne. Then we went to the toilets, where I'd picked up some lollipops and was looking in my bag for some change to pay for them when it all kicked off. I never denied hitting the attendant; I'm from a Newcastle council estate and my older brothers and my sister had drummed it into me that you stick up for yourself. In my mind I had to be that person, sticking up for myself. Later I learned to let go of that a bit and I realized that the better option that night would have been to have said, 'You know what, I'm going to get security.'

I was put in a police cell overnight and questioned the next morning but I wasn't asked about anything racist at the time because nothing had been said about that; I was only asked about hitting her and I was honest and open and told them what I believed had happened. My mother had always said if you tell the truth you can never go wrong, even if the truth looks bad, and I believed that. I was totally naïve. A week later I went back to answer bail and was re-arrested because the lady had changed her statement and was making racist allegations, which really shocked and sickened me. Suddenly, I was charged with racially aggravated assault.

I felt the anxiety creeping back, I felt rejected by the press, and didn't understand how they could write things that were so untrue. People have this idea that you just sue, but it doesn't work like that; it just drags things out and it costs a hell of a lot of money. You just have to rely on your fans to have faith in you. I felt like my career, everything I'd aspired to be and wanted to do, was hanging in the balance. Plus, it wasn't just me I had to worry about; I had four other people's lives to consider.

I said to the girls I'd leave, I'd go if they wanted me to. I didn't want to spoil anything for them. They'd worked so hard I didn't want to hold them back and if it was going to be damaging I was ready to go. Nicola was there for me through thick and thin, she was there on the night and she knew the truth, but I still felt very lonely. I was struggling mentally, I just couldn't believe what was happening. I was having some terrible things said about me, feeling like the nation hated me. And nobody had – or could have – prepared me for that side of it. I felt so bad I didn't walk with my head up, I looked down at my shoes. I felt awful for the girls because it was their dream as well, we'd all been through this experience together, and I felt I'd screwed it up for everyone, but the truth wasn't out there. All anyone knew was what they were reading and it couldn't have been further away from what I am. I'd always got on with anyone from any walk of life, always been well liked at home, and to feel so disliked was shocking.

Drew [Lyall], our old tour manager, was like a big brother to me. I couldn't drive then and he used to drive me back to Newcastle, even lend me money because we didn't have a lot then. He was definitely a big help to me at that time.

The case didn't come to court until October 2003, so it was hanging over me for months. I don't really know how I coped. I felt myself slipping back into depression, I couldn't eat or sleep very well, I lost a lot of weight; the 'misery' diet definitely works! I'd been one of those people that had watched my older brothers and friends go through court cases and stuff, but I'd never been in trouble in my life. I'd never denied hitting the lady and so I was found guilty on that, but I was cleared on the worst charge, the racist stuff, which I'd always denied.

I feel like I'm a much stronger person for having gone through that experience. I learned to deal with my emotions, which was great. So by going through all that horribleness I learned to step back and calm down. Now I count to 10 if anything's bothering me. It was a horrific experience but from every bad comes good and I think I learned a lot, especially about the media, and about myself. I learned the difference between being strong and putting on a front, and being professional. It really did my head in for a long time, but it was very character-building.

KIMBERLEY: The court case was horrific for Cheryl and immediately she became a shadow of herself. From being so happy and on top of the world she just crashed in the worst possible way. We all felt for her. Straight away she was like, 'Look, I'll leave the group, I don't want to jeopardize anything for you girls,' and we were like, 'No way, absolutely not.' We just thought we'll go forward as a group and if we don't get through this together then it's not meant to be. We were right there with her and pretty

miserable at that time because none of us knew what was going to happen. We were in the studio recording and we didn't know if there was any point making the album. I just remember her being so sad. Obviously, the truth came out in court and we always believed it would, but she still had to go through that horrible period. I don't know how she got through it. I don't think I could have.

Life was flat out for the first two, three years of Girls Aloud. Nobody was prepared for being in the band really. I don't think any of us realized how hard it would be, but I think all the work and different things I'd done before were good preparation. I'd done *Les Mis* when I was younger, where I'd leave school, go to the theatre, do the performance, get home late and get up for school again in the morning. I was travelling from Bradford to Manchester as well and that was 55 performances over a few months, so I think that had helped me with the work ethic thing. I just felt it made sense to have to work hard otherwise how can you have all these amazing things?

Living in London was a bit weird for the first year; I think me and Nadine got each other through that. We were really compatible because we were both tidy and liked cooking, so that made it work a lot easier. Our flat was all serene and cream with a plant in the corner: never messy. Cheryl and Nicola were the other extreme; they didn't know how to do washing or work the heating or pay the bills.

If we all had a Saturday night off we'd go to Propaganda, in Wardour Street, which then became Trap, and we loved it. It was our haunt. We'd see people we knew from work and it was just a brilliant time.

Me and Nadine used to go a bit mad sometimes, literally. If we had gigs on weekends, we might not go out for a month, so we'd buy a bottle of wine and put the music on and start dancing round like nutters or we'd sing at the top of our voices. We knew we were mad but we didn't care. God knows what our neighbours thought.

NADINE: I got really lucky living with Kimberley because we got along, we were both really clean and tidy. I'd be constantly bleaching and hoovering and she was the same. We just got into a routine and we had a really good time. It was Kimberley who taught me how to be an adult, how to do simple things like paying bills. I hadn't a clue. We set up a joint account and put money in to pay the bills and buy food, which was brilliant because you hear horror stories about people who live together.

A few nights we had a bottle of champagne in the house, had a couple of glasses, turned the music up full blast and danced around like a couple of eejits in the living room. My boyfriend, Neil [McCafferty], came to the door one night and he could hear us down the hallway singing and dancing. He was like, 'You're going to have to tone it down,' but we were young and working hard and we didn't get out that much. I was 17 so I wasn't supposed to be in clubs and had that whole nervous thing of knowing I wasn't old enough. And West End clubs, if you want a table you have to pay for it and buy bottles of drink, and we didn't have that kind of money. I think people think because you're on TV you should have a million pounds in the bank, but that's not the case. I wouldn't say I had little money for a girl of that age, but it was little in terms of the lifestyle we were expected to lead, but that was good because it keeps you grounded. If I'd been given loads of money at the start, at 17 years old, it could have been a whole different story.

CHERYL: Me and Nicola were living like a pair of tramps. Neither of us knew how to work the washing machine. My God, the laundry, it was disgusting. We didn't know how to cook so we lived on junk, takeaways. We'd get in from work and the last thing we wanted was to start tidying up. We had sweets we'd been eating that were stuck to the floor. It was disgusting, a filth pit, just two teenage girls out of their depth. We were living out of pizza boxes and takeaway cartons; it was an absolute disgrace.

I'd lived in my own flat before but I didn't have anything then, no furniture. I literally had a bed, a quilt, a cup, a kettle, tea, sugar, coffee, and milk – UHT milk, because I didn't have a fridge. I'd always been quite independent but I didn't realize until I was with Nicola that I did not have a clue. I knew how to fry bacon, that's how I put on a stone and a half and was bigger than I'd ever been.

NICOLA: Me and Cheryl were like little chavs. We were from rough places and we completely connected. We shared a flat and I remember when we went to view it we were so excited and we thought we were class because the sofa was red leather and it looked like a bachelor pad. It was so cool, but honest to God, it was a mess; you've got no idea. We didn't ever cook, just lived on noodles and beans and bacon butties and takeaways: Domino's pizza, wedges and garlic dip every night. There were pizza boxes everywhere. We got to the point where the pizza delivery man was bringing us milk and bread, too. We hardly ever did any washing, Cheryl's mum had to come and do it. The way we lived was beyond a joke – I was worse than her. We had no idea about anything. It was ridiculous. For three weeks we had no heating and we were sitting with our coats wrapped round us shivering, turning on the shower and the gas rings just to try and create a bit of heat. Then someone came to look at it and just turned a dial on the wall and said, 'That's all you had to do.' Although at the time we were baffled, I look back at the two of us living there and I'd never change a second of it. No matter how dirty it was or how many unhappy memories I have from then, I also have some of the happiest, funniest memories, too. I wish I could have filmed the pair of us – laughing, crying and dealing with the unknown day after day.

We never used to read our post either. We were living in a block of flats where everyone had their own post box in the entrance and ours was overflowing. It got to the point where our mail was being stacked up on the floor. We were away constantly and so wrapped up in our own world that post just did not come into it and the bills were piling up. We didn't pay our council tax, just through ignorance, and it got to the point where we'd been summoned to court and missed the hearing – basically because we'd ignored every letter we'd been sent. Eventually, the record company knew and they were like, 'Oh my God, have you not been opening any of your mail?' Anyway, it was terrible and everyone knew about it but it was finally getting sorted.

While all that was going on we went up to Scotland to do a gig and when we got to the hotel we had hours to kill before we went on stage. Paul, our tour manager, decided to get some sleep and told us not to ring him unless we really needed him. It was three in the afternoon, we couldn't go out, and we just thought what are we meant to do for the next six hours? We were going out of our minds. I thought – I know. Let's play a trick on Paul.

Me, Kimberley and Nadine were in my room, he was in the room next door, and Nadine rang him pretending to be the hotel receptionist. He was half asleep and she was like, 'I'm so sorry to disturb you but I have a small issue. There are a few policemen downstairs looking for Miss Roberts and Miss Tweedy. It's something about a summons. Forgive me if I'm getting this wrong but I think it's something to do with council tax.' At that point he was wide awake and Nadine was saying, 'There are rather a lot of paparazzi here as well so if you'd just like to defuse the situation …' He was like, 'Right, okay, I'll deal with it.' We were howling, all gathered round the little spy hole in my door, expecting him to run past on his way to reception but he came straight to my room. Bang, bang, bang! Kimberley and Nadine raced into the bathroom and hid and left me to deal with him. When I opened the door he flew in, hair all over, eyes wild, shirt undone. He had his shoes and socks in his hand and he was ranting: 'You've really done it this time, Nicola. Do you know there are police officers everywhere? I've got to think of a way of getting you out of this hotel. We need to get the girls together and get out the back way. Forget the gig.' He sat on the end of my bed trying to get his shoes and socks on, rambling on about finding the fire exit and getting us out, and I couldn't keep a straight face. I started laughing and he just looked at me and went, 'Oh no. Don't tell me this is a joke.' He really wasn't happy and promised he'd get me back. For a whole year afterwards I was terrified about what he was going to do. Luckily, he never did get me. Some of the tricks we used to play, though; we were really bad, but it was pure boredom that drove us to it.

> **The way we lived was beyond a joke – I was worse than her. We had no idea about anything. It was ridiculous.**

I had an addiction to shopping at that point. I would just spend, spend, spend because I was feeling quite down. I'd buy something new – just silly things like a new pair of socks or the same

T-shirt in three colours – and it would make me feel better. I had a ridiculous amount of clothes.

All the time I was leading a double life, trying to split myself in half, be a pop star but still try to fit in with my normal friends. I'd go home and my friend would pick me up in her little car and we'd have a few drinks, go to McDonald's, hang around the local shopping centre. It was surreal. I was doing all these schoolgirl things and I was in a pop band at the same time. I'd be staying in my tiny bedroom at my mum's then I'd get the train back to London and do *Record of the Year* with Westlife or whoever, and at that point I wasn't necessarily excited about it because I had this whole insecurity about myself.

CHERYL: I couldn't have managed without Nicola, even though we were hopeless for each other. We cried together, laughed together and had fun together, surrounded by our filth. I always wanted a little sister and she stepped into the role. There's only three years between us but I had a lot more life experience so I was more mature in that sense, more streetwise, and I kind of looked after her the best I could, but she looked after me as well. I think it was difficult for her to see me going through so much heartache over the court case because she felt helpless, but she was there and we'll always have that bond.

Living in London was hard, it's a different mentality; the people are different. Everything seems money-motivated and everything's go, go, go. If you ask someone in Newcastle to nip you to the shop in the car there's no way they wouldn't, it's no hardship, but here it's a big thing. Everything's a rush in London. If I said something in a joking way it was taken as offensive, just little things, so I was adapting to a different mentality. I felt very misunderstood. I was really out of my depth to begin with and homesick. I felt I was missing out on my family life, missing watching my nephews growing up, things like that. For the first couple of years I'd cry myself to sleep and if I had even half a day off I'd go home to

Newcastle, crazy stuff, just to feel normal. I remember going to a really posh restaurant in London – Zilli Fish – with the record company to celebrate getting to number one with 'Sound of the Underground' and thinking there's nothing worse than posh food. I had a goat's cheese tartlet because I love cheese and it was the

only thing I understood on the menu. It was the vilest thing I'd ever tasted. In front of all these really important people I said, 'This is f***ing horrible.' That night I had a nightmare I was eating goat's cheese and it was disgusting. They still laugh about that now, how unworldly I was.

NICOLA: If I hadn't had Cheryl and I dare say if she hadn't had me at the beginning of this journey there wouldn't be a band now because we wouldn't have coped.

I'd watched myself back on the auditions and I was so pale, the lighting would just bounce off my skin, like I had a moonbeam around me. I hated it and I hated people judging me. I'd put on the telly and there'd be someone saying something cruel, or I'd open a magazine and read it. Normal people don't have people telling them day to day they're ugly or miserable. No one would dream of doing that. Being so young and shy it felt terrible and at the same time I'd think, 'Stop being so vain, you've got this amazing job,' but it wasn't enough. It didn't stop me feeling bad.

You've no idea the lengths I went to just to be brown. I had every product for fake tan. We'd maybe finish filming at 10 p.m., I'd come home, shower and exfoliate, put fake tan on, lie in bed thinking please let this tan work, please let it develop so I'll wake up brown. I'd get up and think I looked great when I just looked a dirty mess with all these patches of fake tan everywhere. But it was brown and that was something I thought was attractive. Before I got in the band I was the complete opposite. I'd go out with my friends and get ready and look in the mirror and think I looked nice. I had this bright red hair and it was never an issue, I absolutely loved it, it was my prized possession. No one could touch it.

My personal life was pretty much in turmoil at the time. I missed my friends and my family and my boyfriend. I had some major family issues with my mum and dad's break-up; that was really bothering me. Things were screwed up at home and you can't appreciate the good when you've got so much bad stuff consuming your energy. I'd be up all night on the phone to somebody stressing out and crying about something then have to go to work still feeling sad and deflated. I hated it because I just needed to go home and be with my brothers and sister; we are incredibly close and we needed each other then.

Every weekend, even if I had just finished Ant and Dec on a Saturday night and had to be back for something on Sunday morning, I'd have a driver take me home to Liverpool to go out with friends. I'd put my make-up on in the car, get there at 10 p.m., go out and have a car pick me up at seven the next morning to take me back to London to work. I just needed to escape. Some of the states I used to go round Liverpool in . . . but I was with the people I'd always been with and I didn't care. As long as I could get home on Saturday night, be with my friends and forget about everything, that's all I cared about. I wasn't just one person – it was like I was three or four different people in one body, depending on who I was with. I can't even say who I was. I was appreciative of my position – I'd strived for it for years – but I wasn't taking it in. It was a complete blur. From getting in the band when I'd just hit 17 until I was 19, 20, my career was amazing but my personal life was horrible – and nobody knew. Me and Cheryl used to sit with the telly off and just stare into space and be like, 'What's going on? What's happening to us?' It was so strange.

SARAH: I was totally miserable for the first three years of Girls Aloud. I just didn't feel I belonged. When I first got in the band I was with someone and he couldn't cope with the kind of pressure it put on the relationship so we split. I started seeing Mikey [Green], who'd got down to the last 10 boys for One True Voice. We were great, like two peas in a pod for a long time, but I was living out his dream and he'd missed out, got pipped at the post, and I think it was really difficult for him. It must have been hard for him that sometimes I'd come home miserable and he was like, 'You've got everything you dreamed of, why aren't you grateful?' He didn't understand that it was the best and worst thing ever. I felt like I was tied down, trying to throw my all into a relationship with him, and it just wasn't working.

I probably alienated myself from the girls and it affected my relationship with them for a while. I wasn't very close to them for about a year and a half. We didn't get to know and accept each other properly because I was living on my own and they were all sharing. Cheryl was with Nicola and Nadine was with Kimberley. I didn't want to be the third person and I was the oldest; I'd lived on my own before, so it was no biggie for me to have my own place.

I like my own space. I've always been a bit obsessive/compulsive, a bit of a control freak, everything in its place. I like the companionship of a boyfriend but I'd never lived with a girlfriend and I don't know if I could, we might end up falling out, so it was difficult, but we muddled through. After a while, I got my cats, Marley and Phoenix, and they were really good company. When I was going through my lowest times they were good friends. They'd curl up, one either side of me, like my little guardians.

KIMBERLEY: Looking in from the outside you'd probably expect there to be fireworks constantly between five girls because we all have pretty strong opinions, but I think nine times out of ten we've all had the same vision for the group and we know to leave our differences in personality aside. Of course you have to bite your tongue sometimes and compromise, but that's part of any job that involves a team. You're never going to get your way all the time. I think we knew early on that if we went down the road of bickering we would self-destruct and we were bright enough to realize that. It was, like, don't go there, don't wind each other up.

We took the time to get to know each other and respect one another. We've never had one person who's been so outspoken or bossy that they wanted to be the leader, because that wouldn't have worked. We all have our strengths in different areas. I didn't necessarily get on the best with Sarah in the beginning because we're just totally different personalities and I didn't quite understand why she behaved the way she did, but the more I got to know her the more I understood her and the more I got to love her. She brings an energy that every group needs; she keeps it interesting and she's brilliant on stage.

SARAH: In the beginning we muddled through and of course there've been hairy times. We just needed time to get to know each other; time to secure our relationships with each other. We've always known our career comes first and we've always stood together as a unit. We would never let anything jeopardize what

> ❛ We would never let anything jeopardize what we have. Even if we have our differences, times when you're like, "Oh, I've got the hump with you," it's never been serious. ❜

we have. Even if we have our differences, times when you're like, 'Oh, I've got the hump with you,' it's never been serious. You can't just throw five girls together and expect them to get on all the time, but that doesn't mean we're about to split up. We've never crossed that line. I couldn't be happier with the way we all work together now. We couldn't be closer.

NADINE: In the first couple of years it all came naturally, just doing things hour by hour or day by day and living by the seat of your pants, that's really how it felt. If we had a weekend off the other girls could jump in a car and drive home, but I was a long way from my family and it wasn't always feasible to fly over to Derry and back. I missed them desperately, missed loads of birthdays, and my friends were doing things I couldn't do – going on girls' holidays, or whatever. I had so many responsibilities in London with my job and the girls and it did sometimes bother me, but only in the moment, like if I was to ring up my friends and they were all out together and I was on my way to *GMTV* at 4 a.m. or something. I remember one time crying on the phone and my friends crying, all going, 'We miss you,' but you have to get on with it, there's no point dwelling on it.

There would be weekends when I was on my own in London, more as time went on and things like *CD:UK* that had always kept us busy, weren't on TV any more. I'd just spend my time shopping and watching TV and sleeping. I'm not really into going out that much so I'd just be staying in, contemplating, being alone. It's a terrible thing to say but you know when you don't enjoy your own company that much? I don't know what that says for me but people say with age you're more comfortable with yourself, so I tried to get used to my own company and have these moments of self-reflection.

There were times when things weren't going well but no one wants to see someone moping around being miserable. Sometimes the work is a distraction and it helps to be busy rather than dwell on whatever the problem is. It helps to put on a smile and go and meet people who enjoy your music and are happy to see you. That only makes you feel better.

I've had a tendency in life to ignore things rather than deal with whatever the problem was, just put it to the back of my mind and keep busy with something else just to block out whatever pain I was feeling. As time's gone on I've tried to feel what I'm supposed to feel and identify what's making me feel bad rather than just burying stuff. I had the death of my grandda and my aunt and uncle all within two months of each other in 2004 and I just couldn't deal with it. I chose to block it out. Then another close family friend who was like a grandmother died, then my puppy died, and it was just constant, I mean constant, for about two years. It felt like everybody around me was dying and it was really hard to come to work. For a while it was hard to be normal and mentally all right.

The week after my grandda died we shot the video for 'Love Machine'. I prayed the whole day and talked to him and asked God to make the day okay for me and I got through it.

KIMBERLEY: I didn't get home much in the first couple of years. My boyfriend, Martin [Pemberton], played football for Stockport County at the time so he had to be up there all week, then had the game on Saturday, and I couldn't get back at all. Every two weeks, he'd come down on Saturday night and have to be back on Sunday night ready for training Monday morning, and only seeing each other for that short time did put a bit of a strain on the relationship. You drift apart because you're not having

enough time together. I didn't want that to happen because I did love him and we were really happy before I got in the band and I didn't know if it was the distance that was making us drift or whether it would have happened anyway. We did make it work for a couple of years, we did really well, but it comes to a point where it's not really a relationship; by the end of 2003 I felt like I was living a single life 90 per cent of the time, and so did he. It wasn't fair to either of us, to be honest.

SARAH: I had Mikey. We were together for about a year but then we were on/off for about another year after that. We kept trying again but we were going through so many really bad patches. We thought we were going to end up getting married and I did want that but it just didn't happen. I ended up dating Calum Best, who's not exactly into commitment, but he was good for me because he introduced me to so many people. He took me out for dinner and to new places and I felt like, my God, I'm finally getting a life. It was never going to last, but he never treated me with disrespect and in a way I thank him for giving me the confidence I needed to go out and make friends. Everyone saw me as confident and bubbly but I wasn't, it was an act, and he really helped me. For a while it was on/off with Calum and with Mikey. I was just too afraid to move forward. My way of feeling secure was to keep going back, which is not the way to do it.

Around the time me and Mikey first split up, about a year after I'd got into the band, I was having a really bad time and everything just hit me. I was at the end of my tether, a bit of a jittery mess. I nearly had a nervous breakdown. I just didn't know what to do with myself. I hadn't got any friends in London, no family, I started drinking a bit too much, and just felt I had to get home to my mum. I felt I'd not solidified my relationship with the girls, my relationship with Mikey had broken down, and it was like I had nothing left. I had my career but I wasn't happy. I can come across as being ungrateful, but I'm not. It just can get a little intense sometimes and some days I dreaded going into work, which I think is the same with any job you do. I wanted to bury my head under the covers and I think you can feel like that in any walk of life. Mikey used to say I was ungrateful, but I wasn't, I was just so unhappy when things weren't going well with him, and that's when I hit rock bottom. I didn't feel I had anyone to lean on, I just felt really alone. I thought if I had to work for one more day feeling all that stress and pressure I would snap, just break. It was like being in a pressure cooker, reaching boiling point, and I had to get away, just lie on the sofa with the cats and recuperate for a few days. I got our tour manager to drive me home and that did it. I had those few days away, then I came back and was fragile for a little while but just got on with things, concentrated on my career, and ended up being on and off with Mikey for about another two years.

> **It just can get a little intense sometimes and some days I dreaded going into work, which I think is the same with any job you do.**

NADINE: My boyfriend, Neil, was from my home town in Derry and he'd moved to London to play football for Charlton Athletic when he was like 13, 14, and I got together with him when I was 15, so for almost the first two years of our relationship it was long-distance. When I moved to London to be in Girls Aloud we were more like best friends having a laugh together. He was someone who talked the same as me and had the same upbringing and it was more about having a close friend than trying to sustain a serious relationship. I was just too young. We were together five years but we split up when I was going on the first tour in 2005 and he had a couple of months off from his football. We just thought, let's do our own thing that summer and see. It was difficult because he was such a comfort zone, such a familiar person, but familiarity changes the relationship and he became more a best friend than a boyfriend.

NADINE: I was always singing, from when I was really young. My dad had always done shows and every Christmas he'd put on a pantomime for a friend of his, a priest, and the money raised would go to the church. When I was three I was in the chorus for *Aladdin*, singing, and waving up at my daddy. Then, in *Snow White*, I got to do a song by myself. I was one of the seven dwarfs, Bashful, and all through the show the others sang together but I wouldn't because I was supposed to be too shy. When Snow White ate the apple I sang 'Somewhere Out There' on my own, and it was a really nice moment. I did some other shows and when I was 13 they cast me as Sleeping

Beauty and there was loads of singing. I've always been riddled with nerves but never wanted to let on because I didn't want to focus on it. Backstage, I'd suddenly have that feeling there's something not quite right with my throat, then I'd get out there and sing and it would be grand.

I always felt that my parents' main interests were me and my sisters, Charmaine and Rachael, and it's great as a child to know that. My daddy says when he met my mum she was this crazy party animal with her short skirts and high boots and hats – just so over the top in a wee small town in Ireland. When he introduced her to his mum she was like, no way can you marry this girl – how can she raise your kids? He knew she was crazy but he didn't care, and then we started coming along and he couldn't believe the transformation from crazy girl to mother. Growing up, we never worried about anything. Money was never an issue and I grew up thinking we were well off, that money's

not all that important; it will always come. My parents always made us feel secure, but when I was little my dad lost his job. Something happened at work he didn't agree with and when he spoke up they fired him. He went through a really bad time and money was tight. He'd come upstairs and look at me and my sisters sleeping and have a lump in his throat, imagining us having all our possessions taken and being out on the street, the neighbours making us cups of tea. He'd seen that happen to a family when he was a kid and it was his worst fear. At the same time he was in turmoil, thinking if only he'd kept his mouth shut he'd still have a job.

FULL NAME
Nadine Elizabeth Louise

BORN
15 June 1985, in Derry,
Northern Ireland

STYLE
Independent, nomadic,
reflective

INTO
Music, family time at
home in LA, travelling

CAN'T STAND
Social politics, negativity

SHE SAYS
'Whatever's meant for
you will not pass you by.'

My dad being out of work didn't impact on us at all because we didn't know about it. My parents kept it to themselves. We'd be like, 'Oh, can I have a pound to go to the shop?' and they'd just give it to us even though they didn't really have it because they didn't want us to know anything had changed. Eventually, he found another job and started to do well again, but we knew nothing about it. I only found out a few years ago.

I went through a phase when I was 13 of having no friends at all at school, absolutely none. Not one person in the whole school was speaking to me. Me and my best friend had fallen out over something really stupid, a ruler or something, and we were both popular in the class and it was a case of, whose side are you on? She got her side of the story out first so I was seen as the bad one and everybody kind of jumped on it. I had no one to spend lunchtimes with and this teacher suggested I should join the hockey club, that everybody had their lunch there and I'd meet some nice people. I was thinking, me, the most unsporty person in the world? But I went. They were practising and a girl got hit on the knee with a hockey stick and I was like no, no, no, I'd rather be on my own.

I remember sitting in the toilet one day and I had my lunchbox with me and I didn't want to take out my lunch and eat it there so I thought, where else can I go? I decided I'd go into the lunch room and just sit down by myself. I was by myself anyway so I might as well be somewhere clean. So that's what I did and it was all right. The thought of doing it was worse than the actual doing it. I just sat, had my lunch, did some homework, and got myself through it.

My parents made a bigger deal of it all than I did because the school phoned and said no one was speaking to me. My mum was like, 'Oh, this is awful – why didn't you tell us?' I was fine, though, it wasn't that bad. It was just a very valuable lesson I wouldn't want to change and I'm glad I went through it early on. I was gaining confidence as a teenager and I found new friends, so it was fine. At that age, friends are always falling out. The other day in LA my niece and her friend fell out and at 13, oh my God, it feels like the end of the world: tears, screaming and crying. I remember that exact same scenario, and it's just part of life. I think most people go through a stage of isolation when they're young and it makes you stronger, makes you realize who you are and what you want and what you're willing to put up with from people; what type of friends you want. Maybe people are doing drugs and drinking and you're thinking, 'I'm not really into it but I'll do it because everybody else is,' but actually people have more respect for you if you're the one out on a limb because it means you know yourself. I saw what I went through at school as a positive experience. And, you know what, I've figured out it's the same all the way through life. That kind of stuff never goes away. Some people remain in that frame of mind from school right through to the workplace.

Q Has your style changed since you got in the band?

A I've gone through changes and I think I'm now coming back to where I was at the beginning. I always wanted to dress up and put heels on then I went through a stage of wearing tracksuits and a cap and I knew it didn't look right on me. I'd wear baggy jeans and desert boots knowing I didn't feel right, but I just thought that's what was in and it took two minutes to throw on in the morning.

Q What do you watch on TV?

A Cooking programmes with Nigella, The Barefoot Contessa and Rachael Ray. I love cooking, things like ratatouille and vegetarian lasagne. When my friend and her sister came over from Australia I made them a three-course dinner and did a banoffee pie from scratch.

Q You're a very frequent flyer – what's in your hand luggage?

A I always have a case packed with essentials so I can do all my primping on the flight: moisturizers, toothbrush, hand cream, nail file. I used to do my eyebrows but now they make you put tweezers in your case.

Q Is LA home now?

A I split my time between London working with the girls, and LA with my family, but Ireland is home because that's where I'm from and I still have friends there.

Q What's been one of your stand-out moments in Girls Aloud?

A When we did *Saturday Night Divas* [2007] – that was the most excited I've been in a long time. I love that show. The girls were like, 'It's another TV,' and I was going, 'No, it's *Divas*.' Chaka Khan and Celine Dion were on with us. It was great.

Q Are you a bit of a girl-racer?

A I've always been obsessed with driving but once I got my licence I couldn't actually stand the pressure of it. I'd arrive wherever I was going completely stressed out, sore shoulders, mind racing, thinking, how am I going to drive back? I still have the odd stressful moment. Once, in LA, I came on to the freeway from above instead of below. Oops.

Q Are you spiritual?

A I'm more spiritual than religious. You can learn something from almost every religion that's out there. I like the whole Buddhist karma thing, but it's the same with Catholicism – do unto others as you do unto yourself. If you put bad universal energy out there it will come back to you, but I think if you do something bad that's not intentional you'll not be judged as harshly.

May 26 2003. The début album, *Sound of the Underground*, is released and charts at number two. In August, the girls' third single, 'Life Got Cold', reaches number three. Amid concerns their moody image might not be what the fans want, the girls go for something more upbeat in November with the fourth single, 'Jump'. It gives them another top 10 hit, features on the soundtrack of the new blockbuster film, *Love Actually*, and marks a turning point.

CHERYL: It was such a pressure to have another hit after 'Sound of the Underground' and we were very aware of that. We were looking after ourselves and had to be business-savvy from very early on because we didn't have management, which, looking back, is not a bad thing, but at the time it was difficult because we were so young. We thought that Louis was meant to be our mentor but it seemed like, once the programme was done, he was done. Our record company was the most supportive we could have wished for, especially Peter Loraine – the Marketing Director. They all believed in us and wanted it to work. When we did the first album, *Sound of the Underground*, and it didn't sell as well as everyone hoped, we thought, what happens now? We didn't know if we were going to get dropped and I had the guilt of thinking – is it because of me the album's not done well, because of the court case?

KIMBERLEY: We'd done well but the industry was on a decline and we hadn't sold that many albums so it was touch and go whether we'd even get another one. It wasn't really spoken about but there was a chance they'd consider dropping us, which was horrible. None of us let ourselves believe it because I think we all knew we had a lot more to give. We had to fight for everything. I saw a TV programme recently saying we were a well-groomed formula, puppets in the whole thing, that the management knew exactly what they were doing, which is so far away from how it was. We felt we had no management whatsoever. For the first two weeks after getting into the group we didn't speak to Louis Walsh. I don't even know if he had our numbers, that's how bad it was. We knew we were out on our own. We all tried to create a relationship with him, we'd ring him, but he didn't respond and there's only so many times you're going to ring before you give up. We worked solely with the record company, we were part of every decision, and we didn't know it wasn't normal to get involved. We were the kind of girls that wanted to know what was going on, so we'd give our opinions whether anyone wanted to hear them or not. We'd ring the head of Polydor, and he must have thought, this lot are mad, they don't understand how it works. We had a really strong relationship with Peter Loraine and we'd ring him constantly and do his head in. Luckily, we had people who were passionate and willing to go beyond their job description to help us. Poppy [Stanton] at the record company and our tour manager managed our diary between them, which we didn't know wasn't normal. It was the most bizarre set-up. We had nobody protecting us and we were trying to learn as we went along. We'd turn up to gigs in our own clothes because we had no management speaking to the record company to try and find the budget for clothes so we'd just ring each other and say, 'What are you going to wear? Right, we'll wear jeans and coloured vests and try to do something to look like a band,' but obviously we looked terrible.

> **We'd turn up to gigs in our own clothes because we had no management speaking to the record company to try and find the budget for clothes so we'd just ring each other and say, "What are you going to wear?"**

NICOLA: We managed ourselves for the first two or three years. It was terrible. I don't know how we're still here. I just felt like it was a game at the beginning, a bit like snakes and ladders, and sometimes you'd go up the ladder but then you might land

on a square and fall down the snake. We had a big profile but our album didn't do as well as the record company hoped and I used to think any minute now we could fall flat and what the hell are we going to do if this fails? It's a very fickle business and we had to learn very quickly – budgeting, styling, you name it, we had to do it. We had no one fighting our corner and we were newcomers, so for the first few years it was a real struggle. We were just normal girls. We had no clothes to wear if we were doing a gig so we looked terrible, but my God we've been lucky. We have got so much respect for our record company because they really stuck by us and we had a strong relationship with Colin Barlow, the joint MD. We didn't know that normally the manager does the dirty work and deals with the record company. We were really opinionated. It was us having the arguments, sharing the ups and downs, and that was really beneficial because we were friends. It would have been harder for them to let us go.

SARAH: It was hard for us to follow such a successful first single. We'd been at number one for four weeks with 'Sound of the Underground'. We were the first band to have a Christmas number one with its début single and the first girl band to début at number one. It was also the quickest any band had ever gone from being formed to having a number one, so we'd set three new records. How do you top that? We didn't have Brian Higgins on board full-time as our producer then, we hadn't found our sound, but I think the record company saw the potential in us. They knew we weren't the run-of-the-mill groomed band, that we were outspoken, ambitious girls. I think they accepted that growing up in the limelight we were going

> 6 We were the first band to have a Christmas number one with its début single and the first girl band to début at number one. It was also the quickest any band had ever gone from being formed to having a number one, so we'd set three new records. How do you top that? 9

to make mistakes, but we had a really good rapport and they were very understanding.

KIMBERLEY: I've got so much respect for Polydor and the team there and I believe it's our relationship with them that made it work. We had the same vision and worked really well together, and maybe if Louis had been putting his opinion in it would have been different. I think a lot of the people at the record company have a genuine care and love for us because of how it was. There's a lot of emotional attachment.

It was 'Jump' off the first album that was a big turning point for us in November 2003. We'd already had 'No Good Advice' and 'Life Got Cold', but 'Jump', a cover of an old Pointer Sisters song, was the biggest single for us since 'Sound of the Underground', and the association with the film, *Love Actually*, pushed the album and made a big difference and really worked for us.

The day we did the video I'd just split up with Martin, my boyfriend. You never plan these things, it just happened. We'd been on the phone saying we can't keep going round in circles, let's just break, for now anyway – and the next day was the 'Jump' video. I wanted to tell people but I didn't because I knew if I started to explain I'd just break down, so I had my hair and make-up done and then I just couldn't hold it together and burst out crying and ruined all my make-up. I had to tell them all what was going on and they were like, 'don't worry, let it all out, take as much time as you need'. I just had to block it out of my mind because I knew I couldn't break down again, but it was hard. I felt terrible. It's difficult when you've got personal things going on in this job. You can't keep it all to yourself and just not speak to people because they wonder why you're miserable. You can't have bad days because you're meeting new people all the time and you have to be up and nice even if you don't feel like it, but those are the times I feel so lucky and grateful to have the other four girls. They'll do whatever they can to make it easier. We all do that for each other.

CHERYL: 'Jump' was a great song for us. That was the point when we realized everything we'd been doing was quite down and moody. On 'No Good Advice' and 'Life Got Cold' we were snarly and moody and that's not what people wanted. They wanted fun and upbeat, and that's what 'Jump' was.

NICOLA: 'Jump' lifted our profile because of the premiere of *Love Actually*. That song was meant to be. It was a turning point and everyone loved it. We were invited to the premiere and we were all rushing round getting ready, putting on long dresses and little diamond earrings. It was weird on the red carpet, all dressed up, people shouting your name, and not really knowing how to act. You feel a bit out of place and you think should I stand and get my picture done or would they prefer to take one of the other girls' picture? Then halfway through the film me and Kimberley and Cheryl went to the toilet and I stubbed my toe on this big, heavy door. There was blood everywhere. I had this gorgeous dress on, strappy shoes, paparazzi everywhere – and a big bandage on my foot. I looked like an absolute idiot.

SARAH: The premiere of *Love Actually* was just how you imagine being on the red carpet is going to feel. There were masses of paparazzi, a huge crowd, and people shouting our names. When you're little and you dream about being famous that's what it's about – flashing cameras, screaming fans. It was really surreal, one of those 'pinch me' moments.

NADINE: 'Jump' went down really well, people loved the fun side of it – we loved it. It was all a bit dark before and we were fun young girls so 'Jump' was kind of where we wanted to go. The day of the premiere we'd been up since four in the morning, having done loads of promotional stuff for the single, and it was dash, dash, dash. Premieres and things like that, I don't know, I don't get much enjoyment from them. We were told 'Jump' was going to be in the film, then at the last second they used the Pointer Sisters' version and ours was in the end credits. We'd had clips from the film and Hugh Grant dancing in our video and we had to take it all out, so it was all a bit topsy-turvy. It was like, why are we really here – just to have our pictures taken? Are we really justified in being here?

CHERYL: I'd come straight from the Frank Skinner TV show and he kept going on about the court case so I was in a bit of a fragile frame of mind, but it was the first time we'd done a ball-gown, red-carpet sort of thing so it was exciting. I didn't go to the party afterwards. I prefer proper parties with all your friends and family where everyone knows everyone, not ones where it's just, 'Oh hi, you're famous too,' so I went home to my squalor.

NADINE: After 'Jump' we knew where we wanted to go so we went back into the studio in the summer (2004) to do the new album and we got loads of songs. I remember the night we got 'The Show' and then we did 'Love Machine' – which we didn't even like in the beginning – all those great songs from *What Will the Neighbours Say?* I love that album. I feel so proud of each and every song. It was fun and friendly, just like crazy teenagers let loose, thrown into a band, and I think the album symbolizes that, just the wackiness of it all. For the first time the songs really described us and captured where we were at.

> ❛ I love *What Will the Neighbours Say?* I feel so proud of each and every song. It was fun and friendly, just like crazy teenagers let loose, thrown into a band. ❜

CHERYL: We hated 'Love Machine' at first. We just thought it was cheesy. We thought we were cool and fresh with 'Sound of the Underground' and when we heard 'Love Machine' it was like, you're joking, you're trying to turn us into cartoons. I remember going into the record company and saying, 'we cannot release this, we'll be taken as a joke. We are not doing it.'

NICOLA: 'Love Machine' was recorded in 18 parts. We were there for about three days just trying to get through this one song. Then Brian Higgins, our producer, put it together and we were like, 'what is that? What's the guitar at the beginning? We're going to be laughing stocks! People will say we're copying McFly.' We hated it. That's how much we knew. We're all R & B girls and 'Love Machine' was so far away from what we were listening to, so not cool. We were so out of the loop, the five of us in the car about to go in and see the top guy at the record company, Colin Barlow, the joint MD, and tell him. It was always me and Cheryl who were more vocal and I was like, 'Right, girls, we are going to stay united, don't one of you dare buckle under pressure.' Anyway, we did it and it turned out to be one of our biggest hits.

SARAH: Everyone knows 'Love Machine', it's instantly recognizable, but we all hated it at first. We thought it was cheesy and we were like, 'Let's go, eskimo' – what kind of lyrics are they? We went into the record company and said we can't release this. We wanted to release 'Deadlines & Diets' and they were, like, 'Trust us on this.' Oh, how wrong we were. The more we heard it, the more it grew on us. It just shows you have to put your faith in those that know.

KIMBERLEY: We all waltzed down to the office and we were, like, 'we are NOT doing that song, it's really not us at all, it sounds more like Busted or McFly.' They said, 'We really believe it's going to be a big song for you, please trust us,' and I think because we had respect for them we thought, okay. It turned out

to be one of our favourite songs and one of our favourite videos as well. That was the starting point for our more quirky lyrics style and we ended up embracing it.

I remember Louis Walsh turning up at the 'Love Machine' video shoot and all of us thinking, what's he doing here? All I remember him doing was looking us up and down and saying, 'None of yous are fat any more, are you?' That's just not something you should say to girls. None of us were ever fat anyway, we were just normal girls.

CHERYL: Our A & R guy, Colin Barlow, was also the joint MD at the record company. He wanted 'Love Machine' as a single, talked us round, we released it, it got big, and from then on we just grew and grew. That was another stage when I realized, you know what, that's why these people have been doing what they do for 20 years, being successful. That's why they still have a job. They know what they're talking about. We learned so much.

LENA
HEADEY

RUPEF
EVERE

GIRLS
keeping it real

The girls go from playing dodgy gigs to rubbing shoulders with royalty and round off their first two years on a high when 'I'll Stand By You', the official Children in Need single, goes straight to number one in November 2004. Their hard work and gruelling schedule reaps rewards as the girls prove they have that rarest quality in pop – staying power.

KIMBERLEY: It was flat-out for the first two, three years, all the travelling we did, hours and hours of driving: pretty hardcore. In the beginning we'd never get days off, just literally work seven days a week doing promotion, drive for three or four hours to some random place for a gig, go on stage, do the set, get back in the car, home by two, three in the morning, and up again first thing to do TV. It was like any new job really – you have to graft.

We were mostly doing gigs at universities to start with and they can be a little bit frightening. We didn't necessarily feel we were accepted straight away so we never knew how people were going to take us. Obviously, you're always going to get yobbish lads yelling stupid stuff, but I remember one time getting coins thrown at us and Cheryl being Cheryl said something to the audience. She was like, 'Who threw that?' And I was thinking, oh God, they're really going to start pelting us now, but she must have shocked them a bit because they didn't. One night I had a plastic cup of lager thrown at my head. I didn't feel like it was a personal attack but it wasn't nice to be on the receiving end. We'd look at each other and it was like, do we go off or do we just brave it out? It's a bit of a tough call but we always stuck it out.

It was always pretty horrendous backstage, horrible changing rooms, and we got to the point where we'd just do our hair at home and get ready in the car on the way. We did our own make-up and didn't even bother with false eyelashes or any of the things that have become standard practice. We'd literally get out of the car, be handed microphones, go on stage, perform, come straight off and leave. Some of the states we must have gone on stage, it's a wonder we've survived this long. You can't sit in a car for four hours and expect your hair to look like it should, and our costumes were normally in need of an iron. The majority of the time we didn't even have outfits, we were just wearing our own things, and that never looks good. Despite all that, once we got on stage we still gave everything we had and it obviously paid off.

The good thing about it was we were all still getting to know each other and having those three, four hours in the car together was a good chance to just be like old women and chat. It made us appreciate touring as well because we'd been doing all that, the small gigs, for a while before we did a tour. We realized we could do a proper show playing to our audience and not random teenagers where probably only a handful listened to your music and the rest weren't really bothered. We put a hell of a lot of work into our first tour, made a big effort, because we wanted to set a

precedent and establish ourselves as a good live act. And once we saw what touring could be like, that was us – we wanted to tour all the time.

NICOLA: It was a real struggle. If we were doing a gig and we had nothing to wear there was no manager saying they're not doing it. We had to do everything. It would be us fighting our own corner and obviously we were newcomers so for the first few years we looked a mess. I look back at the 'No Good Advice' video and think we didn't have a clue – the concept, the silver outfits, it was all just a mess, very frustrating. We had to learn very quickly but it paid off and now we're appreciative because we're stronger and know things about the business that other artists with someone looking after them will never know: you name it, we had to do it.

I'm hyperglycaemic – which basically means I've got low blood sugar – but back then I didn't know; I hadn't been diagnosed. I just had to eat all the time and because we were on the road so much I'd be eating McDonald's and Burger King and pizzas – breakfast, lunch and dinner. I was always asking if we could stop and go into McDonald's. It was a nightmare. It was really difficult because I didn't know what was wrong with me. I just thought I was hungry. I'd be wanting to sleep, no energy, needing to eat all the time. I'd be on highs and lows and feeling faint. Every time I ate a burger I felt better, but I didn't understand they were making things worse, that all they were doing was giving me a quick lift and 20 minutes later I'd feel terrible. We were about to go on stage once and I was in the wings and I thought I was going to collapse. Our tour manager ran and got me a can of Coke and the sugar picked me up, but it was weird.

I went to the doctor a couple of years ago and they ran some tests and found out what was wrong. I'm not allowed to eat sugar and processed food; I stick to that as much as I can, but it's difficult because of the life we lead. At least everybody's aware of it now, though. In the beginning, some of the tour managers were like,

'You and your eating habits …' They just thought I was greedy. Thank God we've got people now who seem to get it. When I'm on the road I do sometimes eat processed stuff, it's inevitable, but instead of having something sugary I'll try to have a sandwich. It's a bit of a vicious circle because if I have a little sugar I have to have more to keep me up … and more. It is controllable and I can deal with it, I just have to be careful so that one day it doesn't turn into diabetes, because that would be hard to deal with.

SARAH: It was all work, work, work and it's hard to switch off from that. I didn't have a social life and I think you need something besides work to feel sane. I'm really happy now but it's only been the last year and a half/two years that I've started to feel at ease with everything. I've only just begun to enjoy both sides of it – personal and work-wise. I really struggled to get to grips with the whole fame thing, being recognized, and everything that went with it. I actually hate that word – fame. I know some people want to be famous for five minutes but I just wanted to do something I felt I was good at, and I wasn't really enjoying it at first.

> ❛ I've only just begun to enjoy both sides of it, personal and work-wise. I really struggled to get to grips with the whole fame thing, being recognized, and everything that went with it. ❜

I hated all the attention. People were selling stories about us, telling lies. There was one really nasty one from an ex-boyfriend. I was with him for five years and he'd encouraged me to do the audition, came and supported me all the way through the shows, then ended up selling pictures he had of me topless on holiday. He was my first proper love: the one person I thought would never betray me. It was so hurtful I couldn't even read the story. I got through the first two paragraphs and that was it. The other stories in the papers were lies, stuff about me with a bloke on a fire escape and on the bonnet of a car. I'm sorry – I'm not that kind of girl. I just laughed at them.

NADINE: It does surprise me how much scrutiny there is, and the things people are interested in, because we see ourselves as really normal. All the attention is just part and parcel of having such a good job, though. We get to sing and dance and tour and do the thing we love, and being under scrutiny is the other side of that. You just have to deal with it.

Everything we do as part of our job becomes normal day-to-day stuff, like being on a red carpet and seeing all the photographers around us. We don't take it for granted, but we're used to it now. It's only when I see maybe a video trail that shows all the madness around us – the crowds, all the people taking photographs – suddenly I'm getting to see it from a different point of view and that's when it hits me and I think, no way, that's us in the middle of all that.

NICOLA: We had some tough times in the early days then we started to get big opportunities, like in December 2004 when we got a slot on the *Royal Variety Show*. That was something we'd all grown up watching on TV, and it was an amazing honour. We were all really nervous about it. We were still young and our style wasn't quite there at that point. We were a bit like lost sheep, really, a bit unsure of ourselves, at an in-between stage. We were performing 'The Show' and we went into choreography and changed the routine and put in all these lifts. There was a costume change as well. We knew it was a big deal, 10 million viewers watching, and we felt under pressure. There were loads of amazing people on the bill, like Liza Minnelli and Gwen Stefani and Olivia Newton-John. In the afternoon we watched Elton John sound check and we were just thinking, oh my God, this is unbelievable, we're so fortunate to be in this position. We actually got to meet him because he was playing as the boys from *Billy Elliot* were dancing and they wanted to meet us, so he came over. He was like, 'These young lads want to meet you. They've been talking about you all day.' It totally broke the ice. He was really friendly, just a nice man, but with star quality. Obviously, we knew what he was capable of creatively so we were all a bit like, are we even supposed to look at him?! But he made us feel really welcome in his presence. That was one of those 'wow' moments.

We heard from the record company that we might be chosen to do the official song for Children in Need 2004. We would ask every day if the call to confirm it had come through yet – we were so excited! We recorded 'I'll Stand By You' for it and the song went straight to number one. For Girls Aloud, being the face of such a big campaign felt like another turning point, like we'd stepped up a notch. All those things are huge opportunities and contribute to where we are now, so we definitely felt grateful and had the feeling that things were changing in a really positive way.

CHERYL: I was struggling in the beginning going from being Cheryl from a Newcastle council estate to being Cheryl Tweedy the pop star. Sometimes I had feelings of being ungrateful and I thought, my God, look at me moaning when people would kill to be in my position. I just remind myself how lucky and fortunate a position I'm in for my age and how much I've achieved, and that the good outweighs the bad. When it's bad it's horrific, but when it's good it couldn't get better. Who wants a life that's good all the way through anyway? I wouldn't. I wouldn't want a plain-sailing life. You have to have the lows to appreciate the highs. I'm glad I've had the hard times and been at rock bottom because I'll never go there again and I don't regret any of it. I wouldn't be me otherwise, and I'm happy with who I am now.

It's nice having money and, like, if my nephew wants the latest *X-Men* figure I can get him it, whereas when I was little we would have had to wait until Christmas, and by that time whatever it was we wanted would have gone out of fashion. When I bought my car I felt so proud of myself I was crying. I bought it in Newcastle and it was a big achievement. I used to walk past and look at the cars and think how lucky the people were who could afford them. Having money is a perk of the job – it helps, but it's not the most important thing to me. It's not my motivation. Success is what counts. We get letters from fans who have all kinds of problems, and when they say our music helps them that's enough for me. For someone to say we inspire them or touch their life, it doesn't get any better than that. That's more important to me than anything material.

SARAH: There were people coming out of the woodwork wanting to be friends for different reasons, but also at this time my dad got in touch with me again. I had stopped speaking to him when I was 17 after him and my mum separated and got divorced and, despite what he thinks, my mum had nothing to do with me not wanting to see him. There was just loads of family stuff going on and I had my reasons. I just felt he was being quite selfish at the time. He left my mum to go through everything on her own, and I think for me that was maybe the last straw really. I probably

saw him twice the year after they split up and just got the feeling
he didn't care about me. Then all of a sudden he started making
contact. I wasn't ready to speak to him and I didn't know why he
was suddenly in touch. I know I still have decisions to make there.
I know I can't leave it forever, but I haven't decided how I'm going
to overcome that hurdle yet.

It does sadden me what's happened and I do feel bad we don't
speak. It's been nearly 10 years and he's trying his hardest to make
contact, doing a bit more than just knocking on my mum's door at
Christmas or passing on the odd birthday card, but I'm not sure
I'm ready for the confrontation just yet.

I can get quite emotional about it. One day I'm going to have kids
and I don't want to think he won't know his grandkids; that's
something I have thought about, though. Maybe when things calm
down and I've got time to reflect a bit more I'll have a chance to
decide what I want to do, rather than feel rushed into something
when I'm not ready.

> **❮** My real friends do understand I don't have time sometimes; it's not that I'm being ignorant, it's that I get swept away with what's going on, worrying about what I'm doing and where my life's going. **❯**

It's hard to keep in touch with people anyway because your life is so hectic. I could probably count my real friends on both hands. The others are acquaintances. My real friends do understand I don't have time sometimes; it's not that I'm being ignorant, it's that I get swept away with what's going on, worrying about what I'm doing and where my life's going. I'm the worst worrier of all. Maybe you can say that's self-absorption, but you just don't know what's going to happen and it's always in the back of your mind that this could be here one day and gone the next.

NICOLA: I bottle everything up, and I know that's the wrong way to deal with things, but it's just what I do. I've always been a bit like a closed book, very independent, never one to tell my mum and dad everything that's going on, and I think they did worry about me then but thought I was just off doing this amazing thing, so I just got on with it. You're in the moment, aren't you? It's not until you look back that you realize how lost you were.

After I got in the band my two best friends who I spent all my time with just disowned me, and that was really difficult. They went cold and their attitude towards me changed. I'd known them growing up, but they weren't friends with each other. I was in the middle. I'd invite them to shows and it seemed to me that they were more concerned with what was going on around me than being my friend. All of a sudden I reckoned it was like they couldn't cope with what I was doing, couldn't handle the fact I was now this person getting all the attention, and basically they disowned me and teamed up together. I was in a bit of a mess but my thing in life is that if it doesn't work out it's not meant to be. Even though I say this out loud and I try to think like that, it doesn't always mean it happens like that. I can be hurt quite easily and I'm quite sensitive. Over the past year or so I've learnt that bottling stuff up can make things worse, so I've tried the other way of letting things out and wearing my heart on my sleeve. But that's not always a good idea in this industry.

As much as it's horrible, I would rather be a strong-minded woman who's had to handle some issues than someone who's been through nothing. I like the fact that I'm a deep person because of what's gone on, that I've learned to deal with my feelings, and now I know myself really well and like the person I am.

NADINE: For me, it's really important to view what I do with Girls Aloud as my work, my job, and to have some kind of life outside of it all. The work side does spill over into other areas because I love the girls and they're part of my life, but I still think the life I have away from work should be something different.

I feel very fortunate to have so many great opportunities through being in the band. I love travelling, I'm never so happy as when I have a suitcase packed and I'm going somewhere, and I never imagined I'd be able to travel the way I have.

I do a lot of flying now because my work is in London and my family is in Los Angeles, which I know isn't normal for most people, but I've just got into a routine and I see it as a positive thing. I have it down to a fine art now so getting on a plane is literally like getting into a car for me. I arrive at the airport at the last minute so I don't have to spend much time waiting around, get on the flight, eat, then put on a film I've seen before so I'll go to sleep and wake up in LA or London. Sometimes I get off the plane, go to work, and I'm busy with the girls until midnight but I can't complain because it's my choice to commute. I might be back on a flight a couple of days later, but it's worth it to have quality time in LA, doing normal family stuff at home like picking my sister's kids up from school, and still doing the job I love here.

I had no idea what it was going to be like moving to London and being part of a girl band. It was my dream but I didn't have any expectations. It was definitely a good thing not having loads of money in the beginning because that helped keep me grounded.

SARAH: I don't ever want to think of myself struggling financially now because I've worked damned hard to get here. The goals I had, apart from being successful in my career, were to have my own home and to make sure the people I love are comfortable.

For the first three years I kept my souped-up Escort with its two-tone respray and bonnet modification and big speakers. I was a real girl racer. One night when I'd been for a curry with my friends I was pulled over in Stockport and this police officer said, 'Hello, Miss Harding, I'd have thought you could afford something better than this …' I was like, 'Keeping it real, mate.' It's still there on my mum's drive, that car, and she's begging me to scrap it but I want to keep it. It was my very first car and it's so individual. One of these days I want to do *Pimp My Ride*. I had a Rav 4 for a while, a little pocket rocket, and I loved it but I gave it to my mum for Christmas, and me and Tommy [Crane] got a Range Rover – my dream car. It's such a beautiful drive, like being in an armchair – amazing. I like to be high up off the ground and I feel really safe in it.

I do sometimes feel bad for my family and friends because it's not the same for them. When I got my new car I was at my best friend's house and I didn't want to boast about it but I was really excited and dying to tell her. She just said, 'Look, you worked hard for it and good on you.'

Our lifestyles have changed but we appreciate what we have. I feel sometimes people think we take everything for granted and I know it's rare for someone at my age to have a nice flat in London and a nice car, but I wish they could see how hard we've worked for it. I always feel I'm justifying myself, same as the whole party-girl

image that isn't really me. I don't think it's us that change. I think it's other people's perceptions that change.

NICOLA: When I was little every year we used to go to this caravan park in Cornwall, and two or three summers ago I had a day off and my dad and them were down there so I thought I'd go. I was so excited wondering if I'd see so-and-so, the boy I used to like, the staff, all that. I expected it to be how I remembered and to be able to just jump right back into it, but when I got there it was horrible. The people we knew, that I'd grown up with and had relationships with, just didn't see me as Nicola any more; it was like I was this famous person and they didn't know how to speak to me. Even the boy I liked – all that had gone. I'd had such happy times there, having parties, loads of us sleeping on the beach, and it just wasn't the same. People treated me differently. I sat on the beach on my own for two hours just thinking. I love being by the water. I remember as I was leaving wishing I hadn't gone back, that I'd just kept the nice memories. It took me four hours to drive back to London and I just sobbed all the way. I expect that none of them meant to act like that and probably wouldn't have seen that there was any issue, but to me it was a big deal and it upset me.

KIMBERLEY: I try not to let my job change things but as we get more well known it is difficult sometimes. I used to still get on the tube until quite recently but I've been told off by the other girls. I suppose there is a chance you might meet the wrong person who's got an issue with you. I did once get on and at the next stop a whole load of school kids got in with me and they were all being nice but there was almost a riot on the train. Luckily, they got off a couple of stops down. I was more embarrassed than anything.

SARAH: I like to think I don't limit myself, that I'm not restricted, because the more I feel like that, the more I want to lash out. Sometimes I want to be invisible because I don't feel my life's my own. When I'm working, on the red carpet, doing signings, whatever, I just switch into work mode, but when I'm not working I do sometimes find it hard to deal with being so recognizable. I like to be in control but I've learned to accept things as they are. I do nip to the supermarket on my own but I'm more aware now that people are staring. If one person makes a scene it snowballs and all of a sudden it causes mayhem. I was with my cousin one night, we'd popped into the supermarket late to get some munchies, and I could see these lads out of the corner of my eye following us. I was getting really uncomfortable and eventually when they came up and spoke to me I pretended I was someone else. I was like, 'Oh, sorry, I get that all the time, I just look like her,' but afterwards I felt bad because actually they were really sweet.

CHERYL: I went through a phase of feeling bad for having nice things. I would buy new clothes and they'd stay in the wardrobe. I kept them 'for good', like you would in the old days. I'd buy a gorgeous dress, hang it up, then millions of other people would have worn it before I got round to putting it on. I've still got dresses with the tags on. I just felt guilty and I struggled to justify spending a large amount of money on things. I've kind of got over that now but it took a long time. It's only in the last year or so I've stopped feeling like that. Just recently I've started thinking, you know what, I work hard, I work long hours, I can afford to buy it, I haven't got any children, and if I want a pair of £300 shoes, I'll get them.

I've never been one of those girls that's got to have the latest designer handbag or shoes or whatever anyway; if I like something I bought four seasons ago I'll wear it. I do have a weakness for jackets and I like big rings, but I'll buy costume jewellery because we get slated if we wear things more than once or twice, so if it's between a pair of 18-carat gold hoop earrings that cost £500, or a pair from Topshop for £3.50, I'll buy the ones from Topshop. I like being independent – I've never wanted to rely on anyone – but money has never been top of my list of things to have.

KIMBERLEY: I enjoy the lifestyle I've got and realize I can do things other people can't and I'm grateful that money isn't an issue for me any more, but because it is to almost everybody around me, I don't get too wrapped up in it. I'm not surrounded by people who are in the same position and have the same standard of living. Other than the girls, the people I spend my time with are my sisters, my brother, my mum and dad, and the friends I still see from school. Seeing how hard they work and what their lives entail and the differences between my life and theirs is a key thing. The minute you don't see the difference you've gone too far. I am quite careful with money, I always have been. When something's instilled at a young age it's quite hard to spend, spend, spend. A couple of hundred pounds on a dress or a pair of shoes is a lot to me. I can't help thinking someone could have a holiday for that.

NICOLA: People can be a bit like, 'Oh my God, you've got all this money and an amazing house and lifestyle,' and we do feel very lucky. Money does help. Obviously it's not the be-all and end-all, and it can't buy you love or happiness, but it can buy you comfort and less stress. At the same time we still have our problems. My stress might not be that I can't pay my bills but it might be something else. As a whole, though, I'm really grateful. I've seen more places in the last few years than I ever dreamed I would.

KIMBERLEY: One of the nice things is being able to treat people and whenever I can, I do. My family is grateful but they don't really like to take anything. I gave my mum my old car, a Peugeot 206 convertible. She's had loans for cars all her life so to be able to do that was really nice. There's no point having money and being happy if everybody you love is struggling.

I went to South Africa for Comic Relief in 2007 with Heidi and Keisha from the Sugababes and it was just heartbreaking. It made me realize what's important – and what's not. We've all seen the videos but unless you've experienced it it's hard to explain what it's like. I went into one little hut where there was a grandma and her 11 grandkids all in this one room. They'd all lost their parents to AIDS and she was left looking after them. She had no furniture, nothing whatsoever. When you went to places where children were sick with AIDS you had to try and hold yourself together so as not to make them feel worse, but it was hard not breaking down. We went to a couple of places where property developers were trying to run houses down, huts that people had literally banged together from whatever bits they had. To them these places are home, where they've lived all their lives, and they're being bullied to get out. It's just horrendous, but it's good to see the work that Comic Relief is doing.

When you look at how little these people have, you think, how do they live like that? And yet in a weird way they seem genuinely happy; all pulling together in the community, kids running round playing. They'd run up to you and just want a hug and the babies would let you hold them for hours. I wanted to take them all home with me; I can see how that happens. It's more than a year since I was there but even now I can remember the face of every single person I met.

When I came back it made me look at the things people moan about here and it's hard to comprehend. I was thinking: why do I need all these clothes? Why do I need all these different things for my hair? Why do I need more than one perfume? I think it's amazing what Bob Geldof and the like have achieved.

FULL NAME
Sarah Nicole

BORN
17 November 1981, in
Ascot, Berkshire

STYLE
Quirky, sensitive, loyal

INTO
Music, horse-riding, food

CAN'T STAND
Kiss-and-tell merchants

SHE SAYS
'I'm one of those people,
I have to find out on
my own, learn by my
mistakes.'

SARAH: I was a real little tearaway when I was younger. I grew up in Ascot, in Berkshire, went to a few different schools, a couple of boarding schools, and was never really settled. I had a kooky kind of upbringing. My brother is 16 years older than me and he's my mum's from a previous marriage. I didn't really see eye to eye with him when I was younger. He was Dangerous Dave in the Monster Raving Loony Party – the one with the top hat and curly hair and the Rottweiler dog – and he'd roll up in a Range Rover with stripes down the side. He was quite an embarrassment when I was a kid.

When I was 14, we moved up to Manchester. My mum's family were up there and she'd wanted to move back for a while, and I think it put a bit of a strain on her and my dad's relationship. He's a musician and his work was based in the south. It was an awkward time for me to move because I'd just started to do my GCSE options at school and when we moved they didn't really have room for me in the classes I wanted to do, so I just thought, you know what, if it's that important to me I'll go back to college later. I just became a bit of a misfit really and after about three or four months, when I'd just turned 15, I left school. I was bunking off anyway, I wasn't happy, always in with the wrong crowd and getting into trouble, and one day I just had one too many tellings off and thought, oh, forget it. I remember walking home at lunchtime and telling my mum I wasn't going back. I think she got in a lot of trouble over that and then she and my dad drifted apart. It can't have been easy for her. I know leaving school like that isn't the right thing to do, but I was very

headstrong and I was going through a really bad time with the move up to Manchester and it was all a real struggle. The upheaval of moving was just bad timing. It wasn't like I just decided to doss and sit on my bum and do nothing, though; I was singing, I had Saturday jobs, and I was doing part-time performing arts. I'd have been doing it full-time if I could, but I was too young.

My mum put up with a lot from me. I was either very hyper or very tired and not wanting to do anything, and when I was little I suffered from attention-deficit disorder – I still do a bit. My mind's always off elsewhere. I get really bored or agitated just being in one spot for too long and find it very hard to feel settled. My mum's a really good person, Catholic, very holy, and she'd take me to church all the time, so it must have seemed like I was the black sheep of the family, the spawn of Satan. She struggled with me and I know she had the best of intentions, but I was a handful. I still am. If someone told me not to do something I'd do it. So I had a lot of trouble with Social Services for a while and eventually agreed to go back to school part-time. I already knew I wanted to be a singer.

From the age of three I was in and out of studios with my dad and he bought me my first electric guitar when I was about eight. I've got quite weird taste in music. I love the big divas but I'm also really into stuff like Thin Lizzy, Police and the Eurythmics. I grew up with that kind of music around me. I was into Blur and Oasis as well – I still love Oasis – and the first gig I went to was Eminem in Manchester. I idolized Madonna when I was growing up because she was so controversial and just didn't care. She was so outspoken, such a strong, confident woman, she was my inspiration. I loved the fact she

was like a chameleon, always evolving, and I aspired to be like her. I used to cry myself to sleep praying that one day that would be me. I never doubted singing was what I was meant to do and I was doing gigs at 16, 17, on the karaoke circuit around the whole of Manchester, belting out all the big ballads – Whitney Houston or Mariah Carey.

I went to college to do hair and beauty as a back-up and had loads of different jobs to keep myself afloat: directory enquiries, pizza delivery, working in a sports shop, bar jobs. When I was 17 and my mum and dad split I moved out for about a year and had four jobs just so I could keep my flat going. It was bloody awful. I was gigging as well at all the pubs, clubs, social clubs and caravan parks around the north-west and north Wales.

At one point I signed a contract with an Italian company to record a load of dance tracks but then I got cold feet because they wouldn't let me hear anything before I went over, so, three days before the flight, I panicked and got my brother involved and he really helped me out, got me out of that one. I was always having near misses, half making it, almost getting in bands, but I'm glad now I didn't because I wouldn't be here doing this. I was nearly in Sweet Female Attitude, who did 'Flowers', but my manager mentioned I was having my tonsils out and that ruined my chances. I'd already had them out when I was six and they'd grown back, which was a bit freaky. When I had them looked at, it turned out that I'd been in a constant state of tonsillitis for about a year.

I was trying for so long to make it. I'd been hooked on the original *Popstars* series and I'd gone after *Fame Academy* in 2002, but it wasn't for me. I got the feeling it was more muso types and I wasn't good enough to hold my own playing an instrument. I was recording dance tracks when the auditions for *Popstars: The Rivals* came along. I always knew I'd be back down south one day but I never dreamed that would be how it would happen for me.

Q Do you ever buy clothes and not wear them?

A I have been known to do that. I have one dress, not expensive expensive but top end of High Street, and it's just not really me any more. I gave a load of stuff to charity after I moved into my new place and there were probably a couple of tops in there I'd never worn.

Q What's your style?

A I like comfortable tunic dresses with cut-off leggings. I hate feeling constricted by jeans on a night out. I prefer comfy, baggy tops with tights/leggings and nice shoes. I'm more of a shoe than a bag person. I can't justify spending a lot of money on a bag. I'd rather get something from Topshop. We do get the odd freebie and one Christmas Louis [Walsh] gave us £1,000 in vouchers for Selfridges so me and Nadine went on a spending spree, bought matching bags, then hit the champagne bar. It was great. They had to kick us out at half ten and shove us in a taxi.

Q Do you like gadgets?

A The first expensive thing I bought when I got in the band was a PlayStation for me and one for Mikey. I like the racing games. I was brought up on Super Mario and Grand Theft Auto. I just loved getting in all the cars and tear-arsing around but I don't like the violent side of gaming. I've got a Wii now and I'm obsessed with the ten-pin bowling. It's great fun and quite a good workout.

Q What did you like best at school?

A I was always more into practical things like Home Economics and Textiles. I loved PE and I was quite good at science. If it was a subject I wasn't interested in I'd sit at the back practising how to sign my autograph in my textbooks and making up different stage names.

Q Do you like cooking?

A I love cooking when I get the time. I'd like to get a pasta machine so I can make it. I'm a bit of a food snob. I eat sushi now and I love eating at Nobu. I've recently got into seafood and I eat oysters now. I still love fish and chips and a good curry or a Chinese. When I go out I like places that do comfort food, like shepherd's pie, so I might go somewhere like The Electric, in Portobello, or the Ivy, although I am trying to eat more sushi and seafood because it's healthier.

Q Have you ever missed an event?

A We were picking up an award for Best UK Act at the TMF Awards in Holland [2005] and I got stranded in LA. I'd stayed on and met up with Mikey and Nadine. We went to Las Vegas and were supposed to be on the same flight back but we got separated. Nadine made the flight and I didn't. I couldn't get back to London, they lost my luggage and I ended up at the local mall so I could buy clean clothes. I was weeping, just distraught. I got a flight to Holland the next day and I ended up wearing one of the girls' back-up dresses. While we were waiting to go up for the award I was bursting for a wee so I went to the loo right at the back of the stadium. I'm there and I hear: 'And the winners are … Girls Aloud!' Our tour manager was screaming for me. After all that, I almost didn't make it on stage on time!

SARAH

135

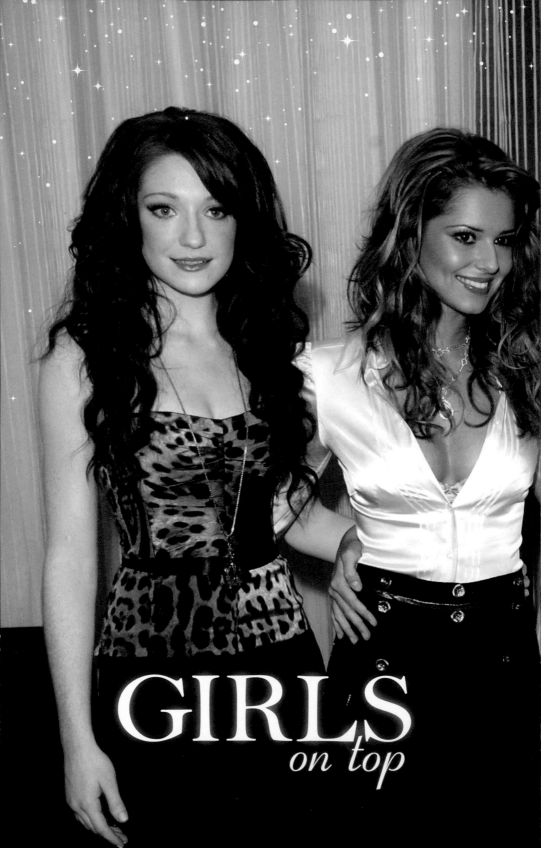

GIRLS
on top

18 consecutive top 10 singles + 3 number one singles +
5 platinum albums + 5.5 million CD sales + 2 Brit nominations
= The UK's most successful girl band ever. So what do the
girls think about what they've done so far?

CHERYL: I think when 'Biology' came out [2005] we
started accepting ourselves and thinking, you know what, we do
make good pop songs. People enjoy us; we're fun, we're successful.
We were getting critically acclaimed right, left and centre, great
reviews in *The Times*, five out of five in the *Guardian*. It was
unbelievable. People like Julie Burchill, who's been around forever,
called our music 'pantyliner punk' and said we'd created a new
genre of pop. We were, like, 'What the hell's going on?' It was
crazy but that's when we knew there was nothing wrong with
us, that we could put the past behind us and make a success of
things. 'Love Machine' had done well, and 'The Show', which was
the first single off the second album – *What Will the Neighbours
Say?* [2004] – did well for us. We were still ropy performers,
though, still unconfident and naïve, and the styling wasn't
right. We knew there were changes to be made, and then with
'Biology' it was like, 'We're all right, the critics like us. Oh my
God, Cheryl got something nice written about her.' It was such an
amazing turnaround and it made everything, even the hard times,
worthwhile.

KIMBERLEY: I think we started to realize that we were
becoming an accepted group, that people weren't just waiting
for us to fail. The 'Girls Aloud splitting' rumours have always
been there, and I'm sure they always will be, but our credibility
and our place as a band doesn't seem to be in question any more.
We've constantly fought to better every song, we've never become
complacent, never wanted to follow a formula; we've always tried
to come back with songs that are different and good in their
own right.

Our style has evolved over the years. We started out as this edgy group with 'Sound of the Underground', then 'No Good Advice' was moody again, and so was 'Life Got Cold'. With 'Jump' and 'Love Machine' and 'The Show' we became more quirky and tongue-in-cheek and enjoyable. Then when we did the *Chemistry* album [2005] it was quite a turning point for us. It's one of my favourite albums. I felt like every song had a totally different vibe and that they could all have been singles. That was a really good moment in our career.

Our relationship with our producer, Brian Higgins, has grown over the years. Once we'd done the first album in 2003 we never looked back and worked with him on the second one – and on every album since. It's very unusual to have this relationship with one producer, probably unheard of for a band to do their entire album with the same person for five years running, but it just works. In 2008 we're recording our fifth studio album and we're still with Brian.

NADINE: 'Biology' was the second single off the *Chemistry* album, and it was slightly more sophisticated but with a fun element. We wore black pencil skirts and got a great new stylist, Victoria (Adcock), who was able to join in with the music and the whole feel of it. It was about us maturing a little bit. The first album, *Sound of the Underground*, was new and fresh, the second album, *What Will the Neighbours Say?*, had a different feel. With *Chemistry* we found our sound. By then we knew we were left-of-centre pop, fun, but slightly on the strange side. It wasn't about structured songs with a verse, bridge, chorus and chorus again; we could play with the elements of how a song is supposed to be, mix it around and have a few different hooks and we knew we were getting away with it.

NICOLA: It's not like we went into the studio and said right, we need to make something completely left-field. That's just how it worked out. We've changed and grown over the years. I loved 'The Show' at first but I don't now; it's one of those songs that does grow old. 'Love Machine' will never grow old. 'I'll Stand By You' will never grow old. I hated the video for 'The Show' because I was fake-tanned to the nines and my hair was a mess – blonde, red, all over the show. I just felt like our style hadn't been finalized, which is forgivable I suppose, but it's also forgettable.

You do get the feeling things fall into place, like we didn't have a single to promote the *The Sound of Girls Aloud*, the Greatest Hits album [2006] and then 'Something Kinda Ooooh' was written – I'm talking last minute, just as the album was about to go – and suddenly we had the song.

I still love the video for 'Sexy! No No No. . .' because it's quirky and different and the movements were quite angular, and that really suited me. It was the first time we'd done something so grand. Wearing the PVC catsuits was like swimming in your own sweat, as crude as that sounds. We had to put lubricant on because if your skin was dry it would rip the suit, so we had this slimy, stinking stuff all over our bodies and then we got the suits on and they were really hot. At least it was the end of the day, so we knew as soon as they came off we'd be going home for a shower.

NADINE: I loved the fierce energy of 'Sexy! No No No. . .' and I really like the video. There's videos you hate, although it's not actually the video that's the problem – it's the look of yourself. I can't think of hardly any times I've seen a video or picture of myself and thought it's good. I can do it for the rest of the girls, but when it's yourself you always see what's wrong, rather than what's right. It's a personal thing, but I just don't like how I look in 'No Good Advice'. When you see videos for the first time, you're kind of watching through your fingers going, 'Oh! Why did I do that face? Oh, why did I move my mouth like that? Why am I such a gack?' You nitpick and drive yourself insane. If there's just one thing you don't like that's all you see, but I think that's totally normal. The moment you're not self-critical you might as well be dead. I do love 'Long Hot Summer' – the grading and the sheen they put on that – and it was fun to do. 'Can't Speak French' was good too and so over the top. You want to see us in those outfits. We did *Ant and Dec's Saturday Night Takeaway* and we were fully costumed, everybody looking at us like we were crazy. You could see us a mile off and smell the hairspray coming, but I love that we get to dress up and call it a job.

SARAH: I still love the hard, rockier image of the 'Sound of the Underground' video. It was our first one, we had no experience, but when we saw it we all loved it. I like 'No Good Advice' too, where I get to smash up the phone box. That's my boisterous, rock 'n' roll side coming out, because dainty blonde I ain't. I've got a T-shirt that says, 'Well-behaved women don't make history.' Funny how the stylist gave that to me …

KIMBERLEY: I still think we have room to develop. *Tangled Up* [2007] has more of a dance vibe, but by the time we do the next album it will be different again. We really don't have a clue until we get into the studio and then things just sit or they don't. It evolves. You have to be a certain type of band to get away with doing the songs we do. Brian writes and produces them but he builds them round our vocals and we bring them to life. I think the relationship works really well.

NICOLA: We step out of the boundary and take a bit of a risk, which I think you have to do in this business. You're never going to survive being complacent. I think one of the reasons we're still here is we've got good songs, and also we were picked by people who watched us grow and know our story. We were just five girls next door who made it, five individuals, all with different personalities to grab on to.

SARAH: I think it's important to keep evolving in terms of our sound and at the same time we've been growing up and finding our way when it comes to our style and fashion sense. It takes time to get these things right and we were learning as we went along. It's about finding someone who can work with each of us individually, get to know our personalities, what suits us and works with each person's shape, and come up with something we feel comfortable and confident in. Personally, I like to make a statement and be a bit more wacky than the others.

KIMBERLEY: We've seen a lot of bands finish and we're left as almost the only pop band. It's a shame because in the beginning we'd see lots of other pop bands and we'd all be doing gigs together and it's not like that any more. Now it's us and the Sugababes, basically. We were at the Vodafone Live Music Awards and it was all indie bands – and us. We were the only pop band and the only girls in the place and we were thinking, this is weird, we're going to look like idiots, but we performed 'Biology' and it was brilliant, a really good thing to be part of.

People we work with who've been around for years say bands come and go and that what's happened with us is really unusual.

I think it's a lot to do with the relationships between the five of us and Hillary [Shaw], our manager, because she's a big part of the band now. And also, there's the unusually strong and familiar relationship with the record company. We've had the same team around us for a long time, like Brian [Higgins], our producer, and Beth [Honan], our choreographer, who's really involved. All the components together keep things turning. I'm sure if one element wasn't there it would be different, but at the moment it's helping us go from strength to strength.

NICOLA: We've got a team that is passionate about the job and we're really fortunate. It's an honour to be able to work with people who are so intelligent and high up in their field. It makes you feel good to be surrounded by great people. In this job, you only want to work with the best. We've got Hillary [Shaw] managing us now. She's a real *Sex and the City* lady – so glamorous, with her four-inch heels and her hair always done and her little dog. She's a real girls' girl, very strong-minded, good at her job, and her heart is so in the right place. We love her.

GIRLS
in love

Falling in love, falling out of love, breaking up, making up, marriage, kids, wanting that happy-ever-after ending … every young girl goes through it, but only a few know how it feels to have their most private and intensely personal matters exposed to public scrutiny.

SARAH: I know I'm hard work, high maintenance, even my mum says so, but any man who can put up with that has got to be worth something.

I won't be pushed into a corner, and maybe that stems back to my dad and thinking he was a bit like that with my mum. I guess as a little girl you pick up on things from your father and because of that I'm always going to expect the worst. Sometimes I push people away or test them. I just don't want people to think I'm a pushover so what I do is maybe disagree with them for the sake of it, be a complete nightmare, want things my own way all the time. I'm very independent and I don't want to feel suffocated. I think I must have been the most difficult girlfriend to the nicest guys and before I knew it they'd be gone. I don't always know what I'm doing and by the time I realize it's usually too late: they've had enough. I'd be clingy with people I really liked and the guy would be the opposite, but when guys were clingy with me I wouldn't want it. I'd be, like, don't smother me, I need my space.

First and foremost, I look for a good sense of humour in a guy, someone who makes me laugh, who's genuine and honest, and with Tommy [Crane] I just felt like he ticked all the boxes. We met through friends and we'd known each other about eight months before we got together. I knew he liked me but I didn't know how much. He'd say, 'When are you going to marry me, Harding?' And I was always, 'Oh shut up, go away, Crane.' I'd never really looked at him like that, plus I was going out with a journalist, Joe [Mott], at the time. I'd been with him about six months and when we split up I was going through a bit of a hard time and Tommy was a really good friend, just there to listen, a shoulder to cry on. He just let me get it all off my chest and one night we were out with friends and we were a bit tipsy and I started looking at him in a different light and it went from there. The next thing we were together and after about three months he moved in, kind of by accident. He had to move out of the place he was sharing in Covent Garden and I just thought he's more or less living with me anyway, so why not move in? Around the time we got together I was still in my old flat but I'd bought my new place and was just waiting for completion. We thought it was all going to be finished and ready by October 2007, and six months later it still wasn't done. It's probably not the best thing to do, have a place done up when you're in your honeymoon period with someone. It just adds a lot of strain to the relationship. We did drive each other nuts but a lot of it stemmed from problems with the new place.

> ' First and foremost, I look for a good sense of humour in a guy, someone who makes me laugh, who's genuine and honest. '

I'd been house-hunting for like two, three years, on the internet, constantly looking, and had a lot of letdowns. I wanted somewhere with character and two floors so it felt more like a house than a flat. In my head, I wanted a mezzanine with an upstairs bedroom, and I wanted to be in north London because that's where my friends are. When I finally saw this place it was perfect. I loved the fact it had so much character and I wanted to modernize it without losing that, make it cool and quirky without it being clinical: a real mishmash of old and new. I don't think I appreciated how much work it would be, though.

The whole place was stripped back to a shell and we started again. We were living in the bedroom while the work was being done, so it was kind of like being in a studio flat. We had no kitchen for three months, just a fridge, a tiny work surface, a little make-do sink the builders had put in and a George Foreman grill. Oh, it was horrible, gross. I wanted to cry the whole time. We couldn't eat healthy stuff, it was either cold food – nibbles and picky things – or full-on takeaways. I managed to get an old microwave off our tour manager. It was a big old-fashioned thing but, oh my God, it was wicked. We could have microwave meals and hot food. I can't ever remember being so excited at the thought of beans on toast. It seemed like the most amazing achievement.

It took us a long time to start to feel settled in the new place. I didn't realize how stressful it would be having all the work done. I wish now we'd rented somewhere while the builders came in and did it because it kind of dented us a little bit, made us not quite as lovey-dovey as we used to be. I think we need to get a place together, somewhere that's ours, somewhere he feels involved, because he didn't feel involved in this place.

Tommy's really only my third long-term relationship and it did feel different when we got together. What struck me about him was he's just so funny and happy and chirpy all the time. His glass is always half full while mine is always half empty. I am a real pessimist, which I know brings him down sometimes, and I feel bad about that. He's probably the most rounded guy I've been with, a bit of a lovable rogue as well, and I love that. In the past I've ended up with some complete losers but then I didn't want anyone who was too nice either. I need a happy medium and I think Tommy's the one. We do have a love/hate relationship. We either get on really well or we're tearing each other's hair out, but I've always been like that, really passionate.

Being a DJ means he works funny hours. He works at Mahiki and if he stays for drinks he sometimes doesn't come home until half five in the morning. That's fine if I'm working nights or touring or something, but when I've got an early start it's difficult. If I'm not getting a good night's sleep I feel really drained.

I think it is incredibly difficult to sustain a relationship when you're working erratic hours and you're away a lot. You get moody and tired, you grow closer to other people, and there are all these hurdles, and then you think, shall I just let this go?

❛ I need a happy medium and I think Tommy's the one. We either get on really well or we're tearing each other's hair out, but I've always been like that, really passionate. ❜

All my life I was so insecure I'd jump from one boyfriend to the next because I didn't like being on my own. I'd be running into relationships on the rebound and they wouldn't work out. I've fallen for people in the past and put my trust in them, let my guard down, and then when the realization dawns I've been naïve my self-esteem has suffered. Most of my boyfriends cheated on me and most of the time they dumped me, not the other way round. One paper called me the 'slapper' of the band. I don't think so. I've never even had a one-night stand. I have lots of male friends but that doesn't mean I'm linked romantically with all of them. I think going out with the wrong men has taught me what not to accept and as I've got older I've become stronger. I won't tolerate certain behaviour, men thinking they can walk all over me, and I think some of them are threatened by that. They don't like a girl with a strong mind and a strong sense of self-belief.

My long-term dream is to have a place in the country. I want to be able to build something or find a nice barn conversion with about ten acres and turn it into my estate. That would be wicked. I love being in London too, though, and I wouldn't want to let go of that. I suppose I want the best of both worlds. I'm hoping to settle down with Tommy and have marriage and kids and all that, but I want to be able to enjoy it and not be worrying about my career. I want a successful career and a stable relationship and I can't honestly say they come hand in hand. I can't even imagine having kids right now, although I do get broody. My best friend's had her second baby and I'm godmother to the first but I see what she's been through and it's hard work. When someone hands you a baby it's easier to coo over it and hand it back. At the moment I'm too selfish, too into my life, which revolves around my friends, my work, my relationship . . . add kids to the equation and it's just not realistic. Sometimes I think it would be great but then I think it's just not the right time. I want to be married and to have faith in marriage again before bringing children into it all.

KIMBERLEY: I've been with Justin [Scott] for nearly five years, which is a long time, and I just think I'm really lucky to have him. He was in a band called Triple 8 and they were on the same label as us and pretty much on the same circuit so we'd see each other a lot at gigs and it just grew into a friendship. I was only just out of a relationship and I wasn't wanting to get with anyone else because he had been my first love and I felt I needed to go out and live a bit, but you don't choose when people come into your life, do you? There was a kind of chemistry with Justin straight away and I didn't understand it. We spoke for hours and hours on the phone and never got bored and I remember finding it weird that he'd come into my life and we felt we knew each other so quickly. I just knew there was something a bit special about it.

At the time the record company was dropping artists, people we liked and had a lot of respect for, and Justin got dropped. It was like pop music was dying a death. Triple 8 had done all right, they'd had two top-10 hits, and suddenly they were dropped. I just thought, God, that's awful. They'd been working for years, had a whole year of grooming and rehearsals and hype – everybody thought they were amazing – and suddenly they got that horrible call everyone dreads. It was scary and made us really grateful to still be there doing what we were doing.

I think it must have been so awful for him and I tried to help him through it as best I could, but I couldn't really have been in a worse position because I was still doing what he wanted to do.

Some things must be quite hard for him, like when we go out people can be quite rude, not really pay him any attention, and you've got to be a certain kind of person – confident and selfless – to not let that bother you. I wouldn't like it, I know I wouldn't if it was the other way round, but he's so understanding – maybe because he's done the job before and doesn't want to be part of that world any more. He does just take it in his stride and never makes me feel bad about it. I just feel I can do whatever I want, and that he can do what he wants, that we're both individuals and wouldn't put any limits on each other, but at the same time we enjoy spending time together. I do think his being so understanding makes my life easy and that's probably why I feel so happy. I don't have anybody nagging me, saying I can't believe you're not going to be back until that time, or complaining if I've got to go away. I just don't have any of that. I see other people's relationships and know it could be so different and I'm grateful.

We're just compatible. Obviously, you fall in love with somebody, that's one thing, but whether or not it lasts is more due to if you can live with that person and be happy with them for a long time, and that's a bigger deal in a way. You can sometimes fall in and out of love, but ultimately if your personalities gel and you like the same things and you've got the same morals and stuff I just think you can last that bit longer.

We've come through some hard times, him being at the lowest point in his life with his career when I was at the highest point with mine. That could have torn us apart. We both know we've got things that are really important to us and there's no point making the other one feel bad about it, so we keep going and survive it. We just get on with things.

I do feel I'm the most happy and settled now and we've got an understanding that works for us. My family and friends love him and he just gets on easily with people. I don't have to worry if he comes along to a gig and I'm not free because he'll just go and

make himself busy. He won't come and stress me out. We totally share everything, which is good for me when I'm working hard. I'm just grateful for all those things, I suppose. We like the same things, music and film-wise. Now we've got the house to a point where it's cosy and we're happy with it, we enjoy staying in just watching TV, things like *24* and *Prison Break*. He'll cook or I'll cook or we'll share it. We might have friends round or go to friends for dinner, maybe go out as part of a big group, every couple of weeks or so, have a big night out, but I don't really mind if I don't go out every week any more.

Trust is really important to me. I've only had one other relationship and that was really trusting and it worked, and I just think that's the pinnacle because the minute doubt creeps in you are starting to destroy yourself; I really believe that. I completely trust Justin and he trusts me. I don't waste any time feeling jealous or worrying about what he's doing and he doesn't with me either. A lot of my friends say we've got a really good relationship because neither of us is jealous, we can go out and have a good time, dance with friends, and we'll never argue about it. I've seen that so many times and I would hate to be one of those people. Obviously, respect matters, and being fair to each other. You just have to have an understanding and be able to have fun together, and we do.

I think he's brought out the best in me. I was a bit old before my time in my relationship before because my boyfriend was older and I was surrounded by people that were older than me. Getting with Justin was like a new lease of life. I'm just happy, totally content, and it seems to be working. He's my age but all the things he's been through, like having a little girl when he was 16, and then being in a group and being dropped, have made him more mature than most men would probably be at his age, but he's still fun.

> ❝ As you get older I think you do start to take things more seriously and think about marriage and having kids and whether that's feasible. ❞

I try to be quite philosophical and just think I'm happy now and not put markers on things. That's why I won't go to psychics – I'm just not interested. I feel like if someone said to me 'This is going to happen' or 'You shouldn't be with that person' it might put some doubt in my mind and I don't want that. I think things should take their natural course.

As you get older I think you do start to take things more seriously and think about marriage and having kids and whether that's feasible – make sure you're on the same page with all that – and that's the next phase of our life, I suppose. At the moment I'm like, 'I want four kids,' and he's, like, 'Oh my God, no way,' so we'll have to wait and see how that pans out.

People do ask us about getting married but I don't feel any pressure because I've got friends older than me who aren't married, but I do feel there's a point where you start to talk about kids and marriage more. I'm not ready yet because there are still things I want to do, and if I'm lucky enough to have children I want to be able to devote myself to them. I think now maybe it was a blessing I did get straight into another relationship, because when you do this job the person you're with is your backbone to an extent, someone you can open up to and expect to care as much, and listen and make you feel okay, and without that it's hard. It's not perfect the whole time but we've made it work and I can count the serious arguments, as in screaming rows, on one hand, so it's not a volatile relationship.

I think when your parents are divorced you maybe rest more on the whole idea of marriage. Some people love more than one person in their life so how do you know the person you marry isn't just another person you love but is THE person? I've always thought I don't want a big wedding, all that pressure, because of my family situation and my parents being divorced. I think it would be quite complicated, but then I went to Cheryl's wedding and it did have a bit of an effect on me. It was a really nice day. Maybe I wouldn't want anything quite so big, but it did make me think the whole white wedding is special. I have moments when I think I'd love that and then I think I'd like to keep it simple, small and intimate.

CHERYL: I was never going to give Ashley my number. No thank you. I wasn't interested. Then I saw a psychic and he said, 'There's a footballer, this is going to be good for you, you must give him your number.' So I did, and I haven't ever looked back. Once I got to know him I knew it was right.

The first time I went round to see him I had on a baggy jumper and jeans and really fast, like within an hour, I just felt like I'd known him forever. It was so comfortable, being able to say what I wanted and not have to pretend to be anything I wasn't, and I was just so attracted to him. We had that chemistry, that oh-my-God-you're-gorgeous butterfly thing. The first time he saw me, before we'd even spoken or anything, he said he just knew I would be his wife. At that time there'd been all kinds of stuff written about me and it was always in my mind that people would have an opinion about me, but he said he could see in my eyes what kind of a person I was.

I'd been single a long time, just dating people, and I was quite happy, but now I love being secure and comfortable and having that no-matter-what friend. That's what I call him. It's like having a best friend there all the time. With Ashley, I loved the thought of security and being married, and I'd never felt that before.

I was so nervous about the wedding. I planned every single aspect, literally. Just before we were married in 2006 I was at the World Cup in Germany to make sure Ashley was okay and at points I was nearly crying, there was so much to do. It made me appreciate the team we have around us and how much planning goes into everything we do as a band. We'd picked Wrotham Park, in Hertfordshire, for the venue because it was perfect, the dream place. When I walked in I knew that was where we'd get married; there was just a feel about it, like that's where it was meant to be. We'd looked at a few places and they were all similar but there was just something about that one that felt right. It had a tiny chapel so it was literally the people that we loved, that were closest to us, who were there.

The only thing was they didn't have a wedding licence so we had to get legally married the night before at Sopwell House, which was the hotel me and the bridesmaids were staying at. It was just me and Ashley, my mam, his mam, and the two registrars at the ceremony. I had on a little dress, no make-up, I was hungover from the night before, and Ashley was in jeans and a T-shirt. We said our vows and cried our eyes out, all of us, including the registrars. So, we got married really intimately, and it was personal and private to us. The next day, 15 July 2006, was a celebration, just letting everyone know, 'I'm Mrs Cole – let's party.' We were already legally married so we could have said anything we wanted when we did our vows with everybody there and I was going to add in 'for fatter, for thinner'

> ‘ We said our vows and cried our eyes out, all of us, including the registrars. So, we got married really intimately, and it was personal and private to us. ’

just for a laugh, but Ashley wouldn't let me. He was like, 'Stop being ridiculous!' I was so chilled out on the day it was freaking the girls out. They'd never seen me like that but I just decided I was going to soak it all in. People had said to us that at your wedding everyone wants to talk to the bride and groom and before you know it you haven't seen anything of each other, so me and Ashley were like glue, we stuck together. We held hands most of the day. I just wanted it to be the best day of my life and to feel I was spending it with the person I was marrying.

Before Christmas 2007, I was really broody, to the point where I'd see children and think, oh my God, that's me, I'm ready. It was all I was thinking about. I would try and plan and think maybe I could still do a couple of gigs if I had a seven-month bump. All that was going through my head and I was thinking, do I start trying for a family after the tour and fit it in around Girls Aloud? I talked to my mam about how I felt and that helped me get my feelings straight and made me decide to wait a bit longer.

I've never doubted I'd have children one day, but I've still got goals and dreams, so maybe in a couple of years. If there were any problems, God forbid, I would adopt or foster because I think I've got a lot to give. I can't see my future without children. Having a family would definitely be one of my biggest achievements.

We've had six years of success with Girls Aloud but I'm not going to delude myself into thinking I'm going to maintain it for the rest of my life because that might not be the case, but once you start a family, it's forever. Once I've had a child I'm always going to be a mother and that is sacred; to me, that's what life's about. It's what I'm doing this for – for my future with my family. In a few years from now I definitely see myself with a few children, just being happy with my little family at home, but I want to be at the point where I can take a year, 18 months, off. I want them to wake up and ask for me, not a nanny. That would break my heart.

I think that relationships are the biggest test in your life; there's nothing more personal, and it's how you deal with things if they go wrong that's the key. The hardest thing is that no one else can make decisions for you. Sometimes you just want someone to tell you what to do: to say this or that is the right thing, but when it's something so personal, only you can decide.

When we did the 'Can't Speak French' video in January 2008, I had a lot of personal stuff going on, the papers were full of it, and the video shoot was hard. Sometimes your eyes can't hide it but you find your inner strength, your inner performer. It's almost like being an actor, and although it's tough in some respects, it's good to have something to get on and do. I look back at that video now and I can see how I felt on the day but I don't think people at home will. The girls are my comfort zone and whatever I might be feeling bad about, someone saying something nasty in the papers or family issues, they're my normality. If I was going through it on my own it would hit a lot harder.

For the whole nation to be looking on and having an opinion and commenting on you, things they don't really know about, is tough. I've learned to accept it and get on with it but it'll never feel right. I still have moments when I have to remind myself I'm in a situation that's not normal, that most people don't usually go through big, traumatic things in public; maybe a couple of neighbours hear what's going on and that's it. People say, 'Oh well, you wanted to be in a girl band and that's what comes with it.' Success, fair enough, I want that, who wouldn't? But fame, having every aspect of my personal life written about just because of the job I do, was never my motivation.

> ❛ I think that relationships are the biggest test in your life, there's nothing more personal, and it's how you deal with things that go wrong that's the key. ❜

There've been times I've sat in the house in darkness with the curtains closed because there's paparazzi outside – and for what? Whatever I do or say is going to be criticized, written about and scrutinized. It's hard, but you have to maintain that you know the truth. You have to try to not take it too personally. The minute it starts damaging what you love is when it gets serious. I can have a blazing row with my sister and slag her off, but you can't. I can call my husband all the names, but you can't because you don't know him. People are too judgemental, but karma works in funny ways. You see people judge you then go through their own thing and you think, how does it feel now? People make mistakes, stuff happens.

I believe everyone should be a free spirit. Even in my marriage, Ashley's a free spirit. I'm not his keeper. I believe in letting people live their lives and be free, so Ashley can have time with his friends when he wants, he can go out when he wants – of course he can. I'm not the type of person to ring him and be, like, 'Where are you, who are you with, what's happening, what time will you be in, why haven't you answered your phone?' I've been that person in the past and I don't like it. I won't let anything change me and make me revert to being that type of girl, because it's not me.

Sometimes you have to put yourself in someone else's shoes and think how you'd feel if you were being judged. I'm not Mrs Perfect, I've made mistakes, and if I'd never been given another chance God knows where I'd be now. I believe everybody deserves chances, but I've been in a relationship in the past where the chances just got out of control. It was like Groundhog Day, hearing the same lies. For a long time, I was low. I'd lost a friend who'd overdosed and seeing him lying in his coffin, 19 years old, was terrible. I couldn't even go to the funeral. That's why I speak out against the likes of celebrities who blatantly use Class A drugs because they're glorifying drug abuse and kids look up to them and think it's cool and I just think it's disgusting. There were a lot of users in my area when I was growing up, and I was so terrified of seeing a heroin addict I wouldn't go out of the house. There's only so much crying you can do, only so many slaps around the face you can take, so many mood swings. So I've been to the extreme where people just don't want to be forgiven and there's definitely a line you have to draw when you feel someone's messing you around.

I don't hold grudges. I'm not someone who'll have an argument and then three months later carry it on. That's negativity and it's not helping anything, it's just eating your insides instead of letting things go and moving on. Life is short. You could be dead tomorrow. I totally trust my instincts and my own judgement and I'm old enough and comfortable enough in my own skin to make my own decisions. It's hard not to let other people influence you and that's something I've had to learn because if you took on board everyone else's opinion you'd do nothing for yourself; you'd be confused your whole life. I love the wisdom of old people. They'll say that everything happens for a reason, that karma comes back around, and you've just got to have faith.

I believe everybody's different, that some people are meant to be together forever and some aren't. We all have different souls and different paths. Society has its rules about marriage but I have my own and I'm changing and learning all the time. I'm writing this in spring 2008, and I still feel there are things I need to sort out in my head, that some things in my life are a bit up in the air, and that you have to go through good and bad times to learn from them. When I said my wedding vows I meant them. I said them for life: for better, for worse. There's going to be worse times and better times. What's worth having anyway if it doesn't take a fight? Whatever happens you learn another lesson. Things are sent to test you and I would hate to be an untested person. I'm glad I've had the ups and downs. I can't hurt any more than I've been hurt, I can't cry any more than I've cried. I've been to the highest of highs and the lowest of lows, so one day I'm going to find my middle ground and be happy.

NADINE: I'm really good at being single. It's just easier sometimes, especially if you're busy, and I'm never in one place for that long anyway so it's a case of where would be the best place for me to have a boyfriend? It's always going to be long-distance. I'm never going to get someone whose schedule's the same as mine.

It was random the way I met Jesse [Metcalfe] in Australia, in 2006, when we were over there doing promotional stuff – just ran into him on the other side of the world. If we hadn't met then we'd have met anyway at some point because so many times we ran into each other, like when we were shooting the Girls Aloud calendar the year before last and he was in the next room doing a photo shoot. It would have happened sooner or later. Even in LA when we weren't together we kept running into each other all the time at random places and you think, God, is this some kind of weird sign? We'd have those discussions about why we'd constantly run into each other and that's why even though we'd break up we always ended up getting back together.

It wasn't the fact we were in different places that made it difficult to keep things going, it was more we were in different places in our minds. I see myself as really young – I was 20 when I met him – and any talk about a permanent future just seemed very alien to me, something I wasn't ready for. He was 28 and wanted to settle down and have a wife and a family and that's really it. We were two people wanting different things and that made it difficult to find somewhere in the middle. At points I definitely thought it could work. I was thinking I don't want to get married but I don't want to break up, but that's kind of dishonest. It's better just to be honest about how you feel, then nobody's in the dark.

There was a lot of press attention when we were together, always a different story going round, just a whirlwind, but it was okay. I wouldn't think the press intrusion really had anything to do with us breaking up or the ruin of the relationship, or anything. I think

it had its preordained path anyway and the press was just there to comment whenever they saw fit.

A lot of the time we weren't in the public eye and it was just a normal relationship. He's a normal guy, I'm a normal girl; we did some really fun things and had some great times. We went on loads of holidays, spent lots of time together. We were always going somewhere new and it was exciting, as if we'd just met. He came to Ireland a couple of times, spent Christmas with us there. We went to Hawaii and New York and Canada – LA, obviously. I'll always have fond thoughts of him and the things we did together and I'll always think of him in a really good, positive way. I just think I was too young to think about settling down and I made too many mistakes. By the time I may have thought about it, it was too late. He had a horrible time going to rehab and stuff and I just thought it was all too much for me. I kind of blocked it out of my life and decided not to be part of it and that's wrong. That's not something you should do if you love somebody. I wouldn't do it to one of my friends or to a family member but with him I did, and that was a regret. I regretted being so selfish about it and so dismissive of him genuinely having a problem. I just didn't want to deal with it. I was in London when he phoned to tell me and I'd just been with him, just left LA the week before, and I was, like, 'What? You're where? In rehab?'

I was working here, doing all the Girls Aloud stuff, trying to nip back to LA to see him, and I had other stuff to do there. My family was moving over so I had to get a house organized and if I was in the same situation again I'd deal with it differently.

We split up for like five, six months. He was really hurt, really upset, and I'm not surprised. Then we kept running into each other randomly and we started seeing each other again. A lot of the time we'd just chill out, watch TV or films. He's a big film guy and he had a cinema screen in his house. He introduced me to loads of films I'd never seen before – obscure things in Russian with subtitles, and *Pulp Fiction*, which I just loved. We would eat out all the time, morning, noon and night, then go back to the house and go for a walk on the beach if we were at mine, just do normal things. At my house it would be crazy because there were always so many people there. He'd start playing with the kids and then any time he was there he'd have to be in the pool with them.

> ❝ [Jesse] taught me a lot about myself and that wasn't easy for me . . . He used to freak me out sometimes, knowing stuff about me before I knew it myself. ❞

He taught me a lot about myself and that wasn't easy for me. He can see through any stuff you're putting out there and he could always tell if I was faking an emotion. If I wasn't all right there'd be no point saying I was because he'd know. He's a sensitive guy. He used to freak me out sometimes, knowing stuff about me before I knew it myself. I learned so much about myself from him. Relationships I'd had before, I'd kind of led and set the pace, and so I was doing my normal thing with him and he was calling me on it, just curbing my relationship attitude. Jesse has some really nice qualities and I'll take so much from that relationship into my next one, just about being honest, and taking someone else's feelings into consideration and treating them as an equal. If you're choosing to be with that person, why would you not listen to them? Their opinion should be valid. That's something I learned: give and take.

I'm really great at giving out advice but it's not so easy taking your own. Sometimes I don't know what I'm thinking. I'm trying to make a conscious effort to be more intuitive and know what I'm about, what makes me happy and what doesn't, what my likes and dislikes are. I just tend to go along with things, do the Girls Aloud diary, and there's not a lot of time for self-reflection. I am getting better as I get older, but I still don't like being alone that much. I don't enjoy my own company, don't live alone, and I always have people around me. The only time I'm alone is when I'm on a plane going somewhere.

I don't feel the need for another relationship – I'm not worried about it. It's not something that keeps me awake, thinking, oh, I really want a boyfriend. My life is fulfilled as it is and I have loads of male friends so I'm never stuck for male company if that's what I'm missing. If someone comes along and it fits into my schedule that would be good but any resistance whatsoever and I lose interest. It's not worth the hassle. It's that thing of where would be the best place for me to have a boyfriend – LA? London?

I do think about marriage and kids but my head's not in that place at all. I just can't imagine it would be something I'd want to do now, although maybe in years to come. I was always obsessed with babies when I was a child and my older sister, Charmaine, was 19 when she had her first daughter and I was so in love, I used to do everything for Courtney. Then she had her second one, then her third, and Courtney was a toddler at this stage, and it just wore me out. I couldn't think of anything worse than having kids now because I wouldn't have the time to dedicate to them. My mum was really good, she didn't work and she was always there, just a constant support. I remember odd days I came home from school and she was out and it felt devastating. The whole house felt completely different. I would love one day to have a family exactly like mine. Mum and Dad have a really great relationship and I get on great with my sisters – everyone just gets along.

> 6 I would love one day to have a family exactly like mine. Mum and Dad have a really great relationship and I get on great with my sisters – everyone just gets along 9

What I look for in my relationships is someone with similar interests, similar beliefs – not necessarily religion or anything – just the same moral standpoint; someone who'll enjoy doing the same things on a day-to-day basis. If you're one of those people that enjoys sitting at home on a day off you need somebody who wants to sit in too, not someone who's adventurous and wants to go off doing all kinds of things. You need someone who genuinely likes doing the same things and isn't just saying that they do to make you happy, because then you know they'd really rather be doing something else.

Having someone with a good head on their shoulders is really important, not into drugs or wanting to be around drugs. I don't like people who go out partying all the time because I'm not that type of person, so ultimately that will never work. Family is really important to me and just trying to be a good person, thinking about what's best for others and not always putting yourself first. I think if you do that you'll be happy.

I'm really independent and I actually prefer having time apart, like with Jesse, because you can do your own thing and so can they and you have something to look forward to when you're with them. You're together but not in each other's faces all the time, so you have your exciting moments when you see each other and it keeps it fresher for longer.

NICOLA: When I got into the band I had a boyfriend, Carl [Egerton]. I met him when I'd just turned 16 and he was 15. We all used to go to this local club and even though everyone was underage we got in every week. We used to save up our dinner money, not eat all week, so we could go out at the weekend. We'd get all dressed up and it was the best time ever. He lived near my friend Carly and one night he was talking to her and I remember thinking he is gorgeous, and it just went from there really. That was it, we were together.

I think me being in Girls Aloud was really difficult for him because he was quite shy. I was in the music business and learning and spreading my wings and suddenly I'd become, not exactly empowered, but this 'figure' rather than just some normal teenage girl. We stayed together nearly five years – we only split up Christmas 2006 – and he was really there for me when I had family things going on. We totally had each other. We had grown up together – from walking the streets just so we could spend time together and texting each other in English classes at school, all the way through to practically living together and him waiting for me to get in from somewhere like the Brits. We loved each other but we were growing into different people. We'd been together so long but we were more like best friends. Although the love was quite deep, we didn't have the same interests. We kept it going because we were really close, but in the end we were just too different.

I'd grown into a mature way of life and all my friends were adults. I wasn't living at home, I had my own life, my own car, paid my rent and stuff, had a job, and he was like he'd just left school. I'm very grown up for my age and it just wasn't feeding me enough. I felt like we were worlds apart. I couldn't pretend to be something I wasn't just so I could fit in with him and that way of life because I wasn't like that any more. I just grew out of it and that's really sad but I think it's how life is, that people grow and change at different speeds and I'm very aware of that.

I seem to grow and change a lot, like every six months I'll be a new person, in a new phase with a new air of confidence, a new sense of who I am and what I stand for. It's just shedding skin, isn't it? I'd shed a lot of skin, and I felt like I didn't fit in with him any more. I didn't want to go round and sit in somebody's house watching telly all night. Mentally, I was too old. As much as I loved him, as much as we were there for each other, I wasn't that person any more. That was my frustration. I was becoming a woman, before my friends were.

I think people go through many relationships until they find the right one. When you're really young you don't even know how to articulate how you feel and it wasn't necessarily something he'd done, like I could blame him for anything. Splitting up is hard and the break-up was really sad, but I felt I'd been growing away from him for such a long time that my heart was already prepared. I think I dealt with it all very well. I'm so morally strong and so on it with what's right and wrong and what's acceptable. When you've had bad life experiences you learn how to deal with things. It's that feeling, what doesn't kill you makes you stronger. Looking back on that whole period of time upsets me a little now. I shouldn't have

> 6 I think people go through many relationships until they find the right one. When you're really young you don't even know how to articulate how you feel. . . 9

expected him to deal with all of what my life had become. He must have been just as lost as I was, but I expected him to be able to deal with it. Both of us were too young to understand any of it. I feel like we went through too much together for me to not still care a lot about him. I will always care for him – he was my first love.

I think in my relationships, more than anywhere else, I am very direct. I know what I want, I know what I expect, and I know what not to stand for. I really value myself. I wouldn't tolerate someone cheating or speaking to me like I'm rubbish. I never used to be like this, I used to be a real softie and cry a lot but I've got harder now and although I liked the way I was before, I know that from now on I won't be a pushover.

I don't go into relationships thinking they won't last. I don't play games. I'd rather know where I stand and if it doesn't work out, okay, but I won't go into it half-heartedly. I couldn't be someone's fling, having them call me when they felt like it. No, I don't think so. It would hurt me too much and I respect myself too much to be somebody's bit when they wanted. Although, as I've been in two serious relationships from the age of 16, perhaps I wouldn't mind having a few flings – as long as I was calling the shots!

I'm single at the moment and I'm really embracing it. I like to be around people but I do like living on my own, having my own space. I'm quite happy to focus on my career and just have some me-time for a bit. I've never had that before. I've always been with a partner, always been part of a couple for the last six years. I'm 22 now and I'm going to live my life full steam ahead and travel and just get out more. I've been single for a few months and I've been having some girly holidays. The only time I'd done that before was when I went to Thailand with Cheryl and Kimberley.

Right now, men aren't even coming into my mind. I don't even want to think about them. I want to be single. I don't want to meet someone and fall into a relationship and then look back and think I've never been single, never had time to develop on my own, that I've always been part of a couple. I just feel I want a break, to have this time to myself to be a bit selfish and do what I want. I do like to share things, I want to fall in love and get married and have children: just not right now.

The way I feel now about meeting someone is that the trust thing is an issue. I feel like you can never really know a person inside out. People do strange things in different situations. I've totally got my guard up, I know I have. I might get over that but it's what I feel right now. Most people don't have to think about someone wanting to sell stories on them or talking to them because they're in a band, but we do. I'm not complaining and I'm so grateful for the life I have, but unfortunately that's the reality for us. Maybe if I met somebody who was also in the public eye they would understand because they'd be in the same position, so it might be easier. I would rather feel completely comfortable with somebody – loved, able to trust them 100 per cent – than be second-guessing them all the time.

It's not just about protecting myself; it's everybody around me. I've got a sister, little brothers, my mum and dad, friends, and whatever is said about me affects them as well because they have to go to school and to work and hear about it. Also, with the other girls, we're like sisters now, and when you let somebody into your life you're letting them into their lives as well. If I put them in a difficult position I'd struggle to live with that.

I feel like when I meet someone I'm not going to try and make something work just because I want it to work. My parents are divorced and I definitely learned from their mistakes. I don't want that for myself and my kids. Why would anybody want to make a rash decision for it all to mess up? I'm a really sensible person and that is not sensible at all. I think marriage and children are too easily achieved these days. Kids are so fragile and easily hurt. They're like little sponges, they take everything in. I can see how innocent my little brothers are and I remember what I was like. I just cannot deal with child neglect and child cruelty, either; it really hits a nerve. I hate it. I'm not going to have kids until my career's over and I've done everything I want to do. I'd rather have children when I can be there and do everything for them.

I want to have my career, be successful, then get married and have children and a nice big house … I totally want that dream.

① KIMBERLEY ② SARAH ③ NICOLA

YEAH YEAH CAN'T TALK

GIRLS ALOUD

REALLY BUSY!!

NICOLA ROBERTS

FULL NAME
Nicola Maria

BORN
5 October 1985, in Stamford,
Lincolnshire

STYLE
Individual, direct, sensitive

INTO
Being with her little brothers
and sister, Liverpool, fashion,
music and being creative

CAN'T STAND
Child neglect

SHE SAYS
'Who you are is special to
some people, not everybody,
and that's enough.'

NICOLA: I always knew I was going to be a singer. It was never a case of if, it was always when – always. From about the age of 10 I just wanted to sing. I would do auditions and competitions. My dad would take me to dance classes, and if there were shows, I'd be singing. I'd been in a couple of girl bands, done some demos at a local studio and it got to the point where silly things, like when I was blowing out the candles on a birthday cake, I'd be praying, 'Oh God, please let this happen to me.' I'd be singing, not even something sad, and I'd cry because I felt such passion. I just loved singing.

If I woke up tomorrow and had to choose between singing or losing my left hand it would be singing, because it comes from my soul. It's such an amazing gift to have, definitely therapeutic, because music makes you feel a certain way – it's like you're in another world. I feel like if I didn't have a voice I'd be a different person. I think I have a lot of music inside of me, so I want to push myself with writing. I don't really get much time to practice and I know that this makes perfect, which frustrates me. Now that I'm single I'm going to throw myself into it and try to develop it more. I know that I have a lot more to give in writing and singing than I've already given, and I know that when I get this out of my system I will be happy because it's not just something I enjoy – it's the making of me. The way I feel about it has increased as I've got older, as I've grown into what I like and what I actually love doing. I definitely want to develop this more.

My mum had me when she was 17 and my dad was in the RAF and there was no money, none whatsoever, but then my dad went to work at Ford's and my mum became a photographer and we started to have a bit of money. I grew up on a council estate and, yeah, it was rough but I never felt threatened by it. I'd go to the shop on my own and be okay, but now I wouldn't send my little brother because he probably wouldn't come back. There were druggies and absolute scallies but they were in the minority and it wasn't anywhere near as bad as some estates are now, with boys carrying guns and knives. When I was about 11, 12, we moved to a house in a nicer area, which I hated. The kids seemed too posh. The funniest thing was the area was only half a mile away and not posh at all! I was used to running around with all the lads on the estate, making dens and getting into a little mischief, when we moved the new kids just seemed boring and tame. I was sharing a bedroom with my little sister, Frankie, but I made my mum take everything out of the box room so I could have that. It was so tiny that, basically, all you could fit in was a bed and a desk and that was it, but it was my space and I could shut the door and I loved it. Then my mum got pregnant and they wanted to make my room the nursery so I had to move back in with my sister, but it got to the point where I was 15 and couldn't share a bedroom with an 11-year-old so we had an extension built and I got my own room again. It had lime-green walls, one of those bubble lamps with fish swimming round in it, a lava lamp, a silver cabinet with green snake lights around it and a disco ball. It was an absolute joke. And it was really messy, really bad. I'm one of those people, I hoard everything: papers, magazines, photos, letters, make-up. The room was overflowing. You

could barely get in. The extension was built Christmas 2001, and I got into the band in November 2002, so I wasn't in the room long.

I've always been a deep thinker and I don't know where that comes from. I would go and sit in the garden by myself and sing at nine, ten years old. I'd write poems and songs about what I was feeling. It was just always there. If I had a show the whole family would come and encourage me and give me confidence. It was a positive thing.

Out of school I was really loud, but in school I was shy and quiet because I wasn't confident around other people or bigger personalities. I didn't really want to put a foot out of place and be picked on, but away from school where I was comfortable I was loud and naughty. I was a little cow. We'd go to the school parents' evening and they'd be saying, 'Oh, she's so quiet and polite,' and my mum would be going, 'WHAT?' My family would call me Cilla – because at home I was like a little show off, singing around the house and dancing, trying to rope my cousins into putting on a family show. I'd knock at my Auntie Sue's door and I'd here them shout, 'Cilla's here!'

I was good at school but using my brain wasn't my interest – I found it boring. I've always been quite responsible and sensible and I worked hard but I didn't necessarily enjoy doing, say, coursework for algebra. It wasn't appealing to me at all. I got my 10 GCSEs but I never wanted to stay on and get more qualifications. What for? Academic stuff didn't feed me or make me excited or happy or stretch me in the things I enjoy. When my GCSEs were done I thought about moving to London and going to stage school there. My whole thing is creativity — I love to make and see the final product, like writing and even simple things like creating an outfit. It's fun. I know some people love studying and go on to be top businesswomen and lawyers or whatever, and that's brilliant if that's what you want to do but I feel school only really provides for those kids and some kids just aren't good at it.

When I think back I had no people skills then. Even two, three years ago I'd have that thing of being insecure and quiet in a roomful of people, not wanting to say the wrong thing, caring what people were going to think, being a lost little sheep. I was a young kid in a world I knew nothing about and being 16 in this industry is difficult because everybody's older than you. I was trying to be all grown-up when I'd only just left school. I've always been sensitive and would take things in and think about them and worry, and I think because I was getting a lot of stick in the media I created a hard persona — like a shield, almost. It wasn't me at all. Now I'm happy with myself; I'm stronger, more open-minded, and I know myself inside out. I'm confident speaking to anybody, whether I know them or not. I've grown into who I am. I had an identity crisis that lasted for years.

Q Do you have lots of clothes?

A Not as many as I used to. I've got to the point of going: do you need that? Do you even want it? No. So don't buy it. I used to buy rubbish and now I buy timeless pieces, like a couple of Chanel handbags because they're classic and they'll last forever. I don't get the whole fad bag phase where people have to have every colour of Balenciaga or Miu Miu. I go through phases with shoes. I like coloured shoes and platforms (but this changes with the season), but I'm more into clothing than having 100 pairs of shoes. I really do love fashion: following the styles, watching the catwalk shows. I just love clothes and the sparkly feeling around fashion. It's fun!

Q What's your style?

A I like to be quite finished and demure but edgy too. Whether I achieve that I don't know but that's what I set out to do. I like to feel good in an outfit. I like to buy quality, not quantity, whereas a few years ago it was the other way round.

Q How do you shake off feeling low?

A It depends. If I've got something on my mind I'd sit and write, or if I needed a laugh I'd go out with my friends. I've seen people get low, and I've been low before so I know you have to get out of it quickly because depression is something that can really take hold of your life and it affects others around you. So you have to be aware and just say, you know what? It's not that bad … and try to get on with it.

Q What's your idea of heaven?

A I love going home to see the kids. My brothers, Clayton and Harrison, are 8 and 11 now, and they're my endorphins. They're so funny you just laugh all day and become a kid again. They see me as an adult in a band driving a big car but when I'm with them you wouldn't think I was nearly 23. They're great to be around.

Q What's in your bag on a night out?

A Everything: perfume, phone, credit card, house keys and every bit of make-up. I've got one of those faces make-up slides off.

Q What great parties have you been to?

A I haven't really been to many amazing parties. I seem to have had lots of good, fun, memorable nights out. I love nights when you still laugh and talk about 5 years later. That's the best. Just recently I went on a girls' holiday to St Tropez and I fell in love with the place. The whole place, I just loved it. Me and my friends had such a fun time – pretty wild. I think it's important to have fun now as I'm still only 22 and I didn't get much of a normal teenage life, so every now and then I go a bit mad and get it out of my system. I dare say I'll still be having these bursts of madness when I'm 30!

Q Do you count your blessings?

A Yeah, I'm very aware that life for others isn't as rosy as it is for me, that everybody has a dream but it doesn't always come true. There are probably girls out there saying they're a better singer than me; and maybe they are, but they don't get seen and don't get any appreciation. Maybe it was all those wishes I made, or it was just my moment – but I'm very grateful.

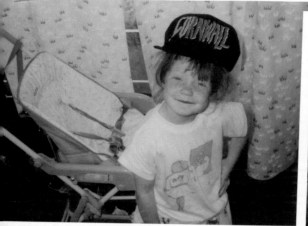

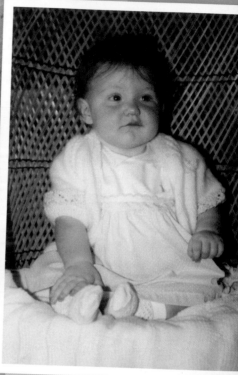

In an office at the girls' record company in west London is a collection of files brimming with Girls Aloud press cuttings. Every day, more stories and pictures are clipped from magazines and newspapers and filed. The press claim to have the inside track on the girls' most intimate secrets. There are 'exclusives' on every news-stand. Sometimes, though, if you're not in the know, separating fact from fiction can be tricky.

CHERYL: The press are so powerful; they can make or break you. When I was going through the court case and stuff in 2003 I used to think that every journalist was ruthless and nasty, but it's not true. There's a lot of difference between journalism and gossip-mongers. Journalists would find the facts and write the truth. If I've been caught doing something bad and they've written the truth, happy day, but when it's absolute lies and then people on the radio talk about it, the likes of *Loose Women* on TV discuss it, every magazine picks up on it and writes their own version, it's out of control. Me sitting at home crying isn't going to solve anything so I just get on with my life, wear what I want to wear, do my hair how I want it, and if they don't like it they can write about it. As long as the Girls Aloud fans stay loyal, that's all I care about.

Celebrity columnists annoy me. I've been offered columns in magazines but what am I going to comment on – somebody else's life? No thank you. I don't know the truth so I've got no right. Ulrika Jonsson, who's had so many negative things written about her, and then comments to the horrible level she does about other people, drives me wild. At the time of the court case – bearing in mind she wasn't there and only knew what she'd read in the press – she called me a disgrace to women. How dare she?

KIMBERLEY: You are exposed and it's not a nice thing. I wouldn't want to be any more famous than I am. I can just about deal with it and it doesn't really affect my life in a way that makes it difficult, but if it was to get to the point of maybe where it is for Cheryl now, that kind of obsessive intrusion, I would hate it, hate it. I don't think it's fair for anyone to have to deal with that where you have to think about every little thing you do and how it might be perceived. It's a weird thing because even people who are stylists or hairdressers or whatever want to be famous now, and I don't understand it, I never will. I never thrived on

> ❬ It's weird that people can have a perception of you when they don't know you. They're basing their opinion on little snippets they've seen. ❭

that, it was only ever a burning desire to perform. Now I've tasted the fame side it's even less about that, but it's not a big issue in my life. Even if they wrote something horrible about me I don't think it would gut-wrenchingly hurt me because I know I'm happy and I've got a family and friends who know me inside out and love me. Although if it was happening a lot I'm sure I'd be affected.

In the beginning, when we were doing *Popstars: The Rivals*, there was a story saying I was this big diva and didn't want my hair done and would moan about my make-up. 'Kimberley's set to be sacked because she's a diva,' kind of thing. That really upset me because I wasn't prepared for it. You just realize how something that's untrue can have a negative effect.

I think most of us were pretty placid and not in any position to say how we wanted our hair and make-up and I didn't understand where that came from. I thought it was going to jeopardize my chances of being in the group but luckily Geri [Halliwell] and Davina [McCall] both spoke up on the programme and said I wasn't a diva, that's not how they saw me.

It's weird that people can have a perception of you when they don't know you. They're basing their opinion on little snippets they've seen. It just annoys me that people comment when they really don't know anything about us or anything about the group. It's lazy and sick, like bullying someone every day. I find it hard to cope with bad things that are written about the other girls. Cheryl gets a harder time than any of us in that area and I always say to her to ignore anything bad because there are so many lovely and amazing things written.

If we see gossip about us as a group it doesn't affect us because usually they're fabricated. It just worries us people might believe them. There was a whole big thing – 'NADINE BETRAYS CHERYL' – which was annoying and a load of rubbish, but what can you do? We know there's nothing going on. There are a good few stories that are complete fabrication and you think it's bizarre, like, have they just picked my name out of a hat or something? They once said I was going out with somebody from *EastEnders*, that we'd been on a few dates and it was getting more intimate and serious. It was some boy who used to be in it, I can't remember his name, but I'd never even met the guy. I'd never seen him out at a

club, nothing, and there was this whole massive story about us. I had a boyfriend at the time and I didn't understand it. Where could that have come from? I haven't really had that bad a time of it but I've seen it with people close to me so I know the difference and it is hard when people are writing untrue things that are hurtful.

NADINE: You think: where did that come from? A few months ago I had a call and this journalist said, 'It's so-and-so from the *Sun*, please don't hang up. Is it true Girls Aloud are holding a press conference to say you're leaving?' I was like, no, absolutely not. I didn't understand. I didn't know anything about a press conference. It turned out it was for the *Passions* TV series and only the other girls were doing that. Things can get out of hand and you don't have any control.

CHERYL: We're human beings and sometimes you're going to wake up in a bad mood just because you do. We're girls, we get hormonal. If I want to be in a bad mood I should be allowed to be, but you're not in this industry. You're difficult or you're moody. Everybody else can have an opinion on you and what you're doing but heaven forbid you have an opinion on anything. If I start thinking about everything I'm going to say, or saying something because that's what they want to hear, then I'm not being me, and I refuse to ever let that happen. I've seen people acting out the way the press perceive them to be and playing up to their media image and I won't do that. I won't say things because someone else thinks I should and I won't hold back on my opinion. If it cuts, it cuts.

When we first got into Girls Aloud we had Sundraj [Sreenivasan], who was head of press at Polydor, looking after us. He's still our publicist and he's become a bit of a lifesaver for me. Sometimes I just ring him to have a moan or a cry, if the media pressure, lies in the press, misconstrued comments, gets too much. He protects us, especially me, and he's become a special friend. He is one of the most important people in my career and in my life now. He's been on the journey with us and he's got our best interests at heart.

Sometimes things just get blown up out of proportion, like the 'feud' with Charlotte Church. I was doing a radio interview with Kimberley and someone called in about Charlotte's single, 'Crazy Chick' and said it sounded like a Girls Aloud rip-off. I never had a problem with Charlotte Church. I didn't even have an opinion on her. I just knew she was a young star. I made some comment about the song, I didn't mean anything by it, then Charlotte said something, and it got to the point where it was really childish. It was ridiculous. Actually, when I watch Charlotte's show or read an interview with her, I like her. Since then I've got married, she's had a baby, and just the other day I was looking at her in *OK!* magazine, a picture of her and her little baby, who is the cutest thing, and I just think what a shame things ever got to that point with her.

NADINE: I went through a strange transition period and became really withdrawn for a year or two, just didn't feel like I had anything to say. You're trying to be the best person you can be but then you have the added pressures of magazines or papers writing things and their perception of you. It was just coming to terms with all that and I think now I can see more clearly. I'm an open book in terms of just chatting to people but when you think there's an ulterior motive or they're trying to find fault in what you're saying, or just looking for bad things, it makes me uncomfortable. That's why I don't want to become part of reality TV shows where they follow you around and want to be in your house and see you with your friends and out shopping. I don't feel comfortable with it at all. That was something I realized, that it makes me unhappy. I can't interact with a person at the other end of the camera; it really changes things. I like to know I've got that distance in order to keep myself sane.

SARAH: You have days when the paparazzi are outside all the time. I sometimes feel it's a real intrusion, like I'm being stalked and there's no privacy. I was in the car going for a facial – day off, no make-up on – and every time I looked in the wing mirror

I could see them. They jump red lights and everything. It's really unnerving and I end up driving dangerously to try and lose them, then Tommy freaks out and I end up in tears.

I agree, there's a time and a place for the paparazzi, like when I'm coming out of work or whatever, then fair enough. It does work both ways, of course, but they do have to give you some space, too. The only thing that stops a paparazzo being classed as a stalker is that he's carrying a camera. Of course I'm going to have days when I don't want to be photographed. I don't mind the odd thing without make-up – I've not really got any airs and graces about that. I'm a bit more funny if I've got a big spot on my forehead or something, but I know they love that kind of thing. Some days you want to be invisible but you can't be, and you have to accept that, so, if you're going to have a camera in your face when you walk out the door and you're having a bad hair day, you make sure you put on a hat and shades.

> **'Some days you want to be invisible but you can't be, and you have to accept that, so, if you're going to have a camera in your face when you walk out the door and you're having a bad hair day, you put on a hat and shades. '**

It's the easiest way to hide the fact you look terrible. I don't always feel confident about how I look. I have good and bad days. At the moment I feel I'm ageing fast because of my stress levels, and maybe I'm drinking a bit more than I used to, but I'm not on the lash every night or anything. I do think stress makes you age quicker, and I'm the oldest in the group so it is starting to worry me a bit because I want some kind of longevity.

NADINE: In the last year or two I've felt the press attention is a wee bit much. There were paparazzi outside my house every day for six months before we went on tour in 2007. You can hear them all talking and you look out the window and they're standing there having a coffee. If you need a bottle of water or some milk and you have to go down to your car and drive to a shop, they're all following you. Then you get out at the shop and they're there snapping away and it's embarrassing. They were nice and they were just doing a job, but that's when it all became a wee bit much for me. I could feel the anxiety rising. It helps having a base in LA. It means I can escape. I do a lot of flying, but that's my choice. I live at home with my parents, Mammy doing my washing and cooking, fighting with my sister, seeing my nieces and nephew. Normality. I fell in love with LA when we went there for work three years ago and just said to my parents they had to go and have a look. We'd almost moved to Sarasota, in Florida, when I was eight, then my sister got pregnant so it was put on hold, so they were already open to the idea of moving abroad. They're in Orange County, which isn't LA, but it's not far, and it's just very homely. We have a house right on the beach and you can tell the sea air is good for you. It's a whole different lifestyle. There's a colour about LA, a specific brightness that you don't get anywhere else in the world, and the weather's beautiful the whole year round. It's just nice to get away, to switch off and be a kid again.

NICOLA: You never know if paparazzi are going to jump out and, believe me, I had the worst picture taken of me on my doorstep. I had a man coming over to fix a wardrobe and I'd slept in. The doorbell went, woke me up, I literally threw on my tracksuit bottoms and ran down the stairs to let him in. I hadn't been in the bathroom to wash my face or anything. I opened the door and there was this click click click and some guy snapping away. I just shut the door and ran upstairs to look in the mirror and see what the damage was. And yes, there was damage – a whole head full! Normally my hair's all over my face but this one day it needed washing so I'd clipped my fringe back. I had bad skin at that time and no mascara on so I had no eyes. The guy had been waiting there with the wardrobe man – not fair. Then the next day, lo and behold, it was there in the newspaper. Sundraj called and he said, 'I'm not gonna lie, it's bad.' I thought, well, it's done now, so stuff it. I get it that I don't look great first thing in the morning, it's just a little weird that the whole nation knows it now, too.

CHERYL: You've got to be a strong character and a specific kind of person to deal with the criticism and rejection and all the

unnecessary scrutinizing that comes with this job, like what colour your hair is this week – all the stupid stuff girls worry about anyway. Magazines have so much power and responsibility and I don't think they realize. They should use it to teach kids about things that are relative to life rather than gossiping about who's got a bit of cellulite on their bum.

KIMBERLEY: The smallest, most insignificant things seem to be the most interesting to the press and I'll never understand that. I'm not particularly into the whole gossip movement we've got in this country where you're obsessed with

189

knowing what's going on in everybody's relationships: how much they weigh, how they're going to have their hair next week, and all that. Scrutinizing people and ringing a tiny bit of cellulite like it's a terrible thing is cruel; every woman in the world has cellulite.

I don't think I'm that much more conscious of how I look now than I was before the band. I've always wanted to look my best and, like most girls, been on a diet every other week, but in a lot of ways I'm quite happy with myself. When it comes down to it, you still want to live a normal life, go out and have dinner with your friends, stay in and eat junk with your boyfriend. I'm not vain enough to sacrifice living my life to be an adored, perfectly toned person, because that's not me. I'm normal – not huge, not tiny – and 90 per cent of the time I'm happy with that. I think if you're happy with yourself you don't feel the need to constantly be proving, 'Look how pretty I am, look how amazing I am, look how thin I am.' You're just happy with who you are as a person.

When I was growing up it was the likes of Kate Moss in all the magazines and I just thought, I'm not that shape, I'll never be like that, and accepted it, but I did know girls who would diet to try and achieve that look. Now it's a million times worse. I'll sometimes pick up a magazine and see somebody who's a size 10/12 and maybe slightly curvy being labelled fat. What's a young girl who's that size or bigger going to start thinking about herself? Sometimes I think I'm glad I'm not skinny. It's good that girls can look at me and think, 'Well, she's a normal size and it's all right. It's all right to have a big bum.'

NADINE: The downside of fame is that sometimes there can be a pressure to do the right thing, or what other people perceive as the right thing. If you don't agree you're stupid or self-obsessed, or whatever it may be, but you can only really do what's right for you. You're not allowed to make mistakes when you're famous, you're not allowed to be anything less than perfect the whole time – not perfect in your eyes, but in other people's.

Things can get out of hand in the way you're expected to live up to superhuman standards.

I have a younger sister, Rachael, two nieces and a nephew, and I try to be a role model for them anyway, just try to do the right thing and show them a good example. You want to be the best you can be. It was funny for me and Nicola when we got in the band because we were so young, 16, 17, and at that age you're still looking for a role model yourself. I knew nothing outside of being at home and my parents telling me what to do – 'You can't go out, we're picking you up at 12, this is when you'll have your dinner.' I went from that to having to be an adult, pay rent for an apartment, get up and go to work, and think about the lives and careers of four other people.

SARAH: I didn't want to be a role model, I never signed up for that, but it happened. I like to go out and drink but no more than the next person my age. I did go through a phase of clubbing a lot but I was single and what else do you do? I don't go to clubs that much now. I'd rather sit in with my boyfriend and have a glass of wine. I've got this reputation as a hardcore party animal and I know I let my hair down once in a while – that's my way of letting off steam – but I'm not a caner every night of the week. I can't do it every night. I've got better things to do. I've got my job to think about and my health would suffer. I did play up to it for a while, thinking all right, bring it on, let's have a laugh, but now it's boring. When I've had a few I become a bit of an exhibitionist, a bit lairy, and then you have the papers saying I'm a bad role model for kids. You can't ever win. I got cussed in some paper saying people like me glamorize booze, like I'm the cause of kids today being binge drinkers. Hang on – don't pick on me. I would never start drinking if children were there. I'm over 18, I'm allowed to have a drink, and I shouldn't have to change who I am. I'm really adamant about that. I've got to make my mistakes otherwise I'll just regret not living. The drinking thing has become my caricature but there are loads of people who are far worse. Look at Pete Doherty. Look at Amy Winehouse.

KIMBERLEY: I don't think any of us were comfortable in the beginning being role models because we all felt quite young ourselves. You don't want to step a foot wrong but at the same time going out and drinking with your friends doesn't seem like a really terrible thing to do. We're only human and we've got to live our lives. We can only try to do everything right but we can't promise that's always going to be the case; we're going to make mistakes. It's weird and I don't really know how people see us because when you're so involved you can't really get a true perspective.

A lot of people say I've changed but they all seem to say it's for the better. I think I've grown up and become more confident. I wasn't exactly wet but I was almost too placid and didn't like confrontation at all. In my own friendship group at school I was a bit cocky, but when I got in the group I sometimes felt I could be walked all over because I didn't dare say anything and I could be swayed by other people's opinions. I learned to stick up for myself a bit more and not be scared of confrontation, not scared of voicing my opinion, and I suppose I got that from some of the other girls.

NICOLA: I'm quite sensitive, I have a good heart, and I was just a kid when all this started so I was like a sponge, soaking up all the comments about me. I was called horrible things when I was 16 and made to feel inadequate, and after being so confident I ended up at rock bottom. When people in the industry say horrible things about you the weird thing is you value those opinions because that's the industry you aspire to succeed in. In the beginning I was trying to be a people pleaser – part of Girls Aloud and, at the same time, the girl I was before I got in the band – so I just wasn't being myself. The two things clashed. If I'd come into the business at the age I am now – 22, 23 – I might not have had the same insecurities, so I think you should know yourself, be your own person. It's an industry full of rejection and that's hard

to deal with. My little sister loves to sing and I would never want her confidence to be flattened and for her to feel worthless or ugly. Something I still find strange is how a grown-up woman or man could sit and write 'ugly' about a 16-year-old child, knowing that that child could then read it. I think that they looked the fools, not me. I'm not going to lie, all that scrutinising did make me feel insecure about the way I looked and acted, and just who I was, but the feeling has definitely eased over time. It's very easy for your mind to be chewed up by this business, so anyone wanting to do it needs to think very carefully. I wouldn't want someone I love to go through what I did, but at the same time it's made me who I am. However clichéd that might sound, it's true.

go **GIRLS**

May 2005. At the Royal Concert Hall in Nottingham, the girls kick off their first tour, 'What Will the Neighbours Say?' They play to around 60,000 fans at theatres across the UK from Brighton to Belfast. In May 2006, they're on the road again with their first arena tour, 'Chemistry'. The audience swells to 100,000. One year on, in May 2007, it's 'The Sound of Girls Aloud: The Greatest Hits Tour': 15 venues, 150,000 fans. In Newcastle, they play to more than 22,000 people over two nights and set a new box office record for a girl band. On 3 May 2008, 'Tangled Up' opens in Belfast. It's their biggest tour ever: 24 dates and 300,000 fans.

CHERYL: The highlight of this whole experience for me is touring. It gets better every time. That's when you see the people who appreciate what you do: the ones who believe in you. The amount of letters we get from people – unbelievable stories about how we've inspired them – and that makes us feel very, very privileged. It makes me think, you know what, that's what makes it worthwhile. We've got the most amazing fans, so loyal. If it wasn't for them I wouldn't be in the industry, to be honest. Music is so powerful; it can change your mood, your way of thinking. I know how it makes me feel and it's hard to wrap your head around us having that effect on other people. To even think you've made one person feel better or helped them along is amazing.

NICOLA: I'd love to be able to step out of it and be a fan. We get letters from fans who confide in us, tell us things they wouldn't tell anyone else, how they've had horrible times in their life, and our music helps them. A lot of them say they've put our album on and for that hour they're happy, and you can't ask for more than that. You can't hope to make anybody feel any better. I know what it's like; I play music if I'm feeling a certain way, and the fact we're doing that for other people is weird. It's like they feel so close to us and we help them escape for a while.

SARAH: I love touring, that feeling of going to new places and seeing new people, being part of a 'family' on the road. It's like a travelling circus and you have the most amazing bond with the people you're working with. I almost get possessed when I'm on stage, just get really hyper and say things I don't mean, or speak over the other girls. I just become that lairy character everyone expects me to be. Opening night is never going to be my best. I tend to get out of breath with nerves and I have to concentrate really hard on remembering the routines. I'm definitely a better singer than I am a dancer, but after about three or four shows it all slips into place and it's fine. I love being on stage, I just feel like I was born to perform. I'm like a firecracker, feeding off the energy in the audience. If there's someone special out there, friends or family, that's my incentive to prove myself.

NICOLA: On stage I can get quite emotional, it kind of hits home a bit, especially with a slow song or a special moment. I love being around all the people we work with, people who are our friends now. In dress rehearsal on the 'Tangled Up' tour this year it was so weird because it was the first time we'd done the show in our outfits and I could see Beth, our choreographer, crying. Seeing her idea come to life made her so proud and that made me burst out crying. I love passionate people, and seeing people proud of what they've achieved gives me goosebumps.

The first night is really overwhelming; it's that feeling of having put together the show and being so moved by it. It's a big thing: everything we've aspired to. You know you're going out to a crowd that wants you to do well and be amazing and that whatever you do they're going to love it, and you just feel so many emotions. Sometimes the only way you can release the tension is to break down. When we're on tour that's where we feel at home. It's a form of expressing who you are. I'm totally aware that the Girls Aloud world isn't real, it's like fairyland, but I love it. Normal women don't hang in the air dressed in Superwoman outfits and capes

like we did for the opening of 'Tangled Up'. I looked at Sarah on the opening night in Belfast and she had this really dramatic look on her face and it just made me laugh. Sometimes, if you stop and think about what we actually do, it's mad. For some reason we can get away with it, but sometimes I think we're not right in our heads.

I love performing, but I never used to as I didn't know how to – I was a singer and that was it. Now I'm excited to grow as a performer. I had a real moment of 'I can't believe what I've achieved' this year. I felt so proud of us, our dancers, our band, our choreographer and just everyone who had worked so hard to put the show together. I felt like saying, 'Take that, haters!' to all of the people who were ever negative.

SARAH: I love the dressing up, getting ready to go on, having my make-up done, the costumes, the big hair. It really changes how you feel. That's when you get into character. As soon as I got my hair done for 'Tangled Up' I felt sexy and womanly, ready to go on stage and strut about. Once I'm out there I'm a different person.

KIMBERLEY: I just feel a massive grin come over my face looking out at that many people all smiling and excited. I've seen grown men on their phones going mental and you just want to give back to them what they're giving you. Sometimes I just wish I could be in the crowd to feel what it's like. It's like you're in a bubble when you're on tour and it sounds cheesy but everybody involved, from styling and hair and make-up to the dancers, the band and Beth, our choreographer, becomes like a family for that period of time.

The tours are so big now: so many people involved, huge stage sets. It's weird to think we've progressed to the point that we can sell out huge arenas. For 'Tangled Up', more than double the amount of people bought tickets than did for the 'Greatest Hits' tour the year before, which is just amazing. I never expected that. It feels more grown up now and I'd like to think we're more polished, that the stage sets and costumes have stepped up a level, and there are lots of wow factors to keep the adrenalin going.

It was just before we did the first tour in 2005 that our manager, Hillary Shaw, came on board. Up until then we'd been managing ourselves, but we were getting bigger as a band and the demands on us were becoming much greater and we just couldn't handle it any more. People were approaching the record company and coming to us personally, and I remember meeting some random agent about something and feeling totally out of my depth. There were amazing offers coming through and we had no one looking after us. We wanted someone who'd represent us, do what we all assumed Louis Walsh should have been doing, and find us merchandising deals or book more gigs for us, or whatever. The situation we were in was ridiculous. Louis tried to bring in someone who he was working with on *X Factor* at the time. He wanted to change everything and we just weren't having it. So we parted company before we even started! We asked the record company if they knew of anyone and Peter Loraine, who's now

the head of our label, suggested Hillary. He'd been involved
with Bananarama when he was really young, when Hillary was
managing them. It was just such a relief when we met her, like we
had a connection right away, and she understood where we were
coming from. It was a tough job for her to take on because we'd
been used to not having management, but she's a really strong
woman and she just got in there and did what needed to be done.
I love her and I'm so glad it was her who came in because she's
part of the gang, a real character. She's got strength but she's
also understanding and very good at managing five different
personalities. I think she's done an amazing job.

NICOLA: Basically, when it came to the first tour, we were
on our own. Sorting out the diary was fine, we could handle that,
but putting on a UK tour? It just wasn't going to happen. That's
when Hillary came on board. It was strange because we were so
used to not being told what to do so we had our guard up. We were
scared of someone coming in and making the wrong decisions, but
we just learned to respect her and accept that she was there to help
us, and that we absolutely needed her. We've got an amazing team.
Angela [O'Connor], Hillary's number two, is very strong-minded
and we really take on board her opinions and respect what she
has to say because she's so good at her job and very morally
correct. And Lily [England], our PA – I don't know what I'd do
without her.

NADINE: It's really handy having Hillary because she can
relate to the simple problems a woman may have on any given day
and sympathize. With Girls Aloud it's all women working hard
together to prove you can have a great career and a great life and
you don't have to be nasty in order to achieve it. Hillary's job can't
be easy, but she enjoys it and works hard and I'm very thankful
she's on board.

SARAH: Louis wasn't hands-on, and at the end of the
day I think he accepted he wasn't doing enough for us. We had

the support of the record company but we didn't feel we had management behind us as a driving force. Although we were working damn hard the money isn't necessarily in the records, so we needed someone to bring in endorsements and push that side of things. I think Hillary must have seen the potential in us. She'd worked with Bananarama and was good with girls and I think we saw her as a bit of

> **❝ With Girls Aloud it's all women working hard together to prove you can have a great career and a great life and you don't have to be nasty in order to achieve it. ❞**

a ray of light when she came on board. We really needed her to mastermind the first tour for us because we didn't know where to start, and it's not the record company's job to sort out the tour.

CHERYL: We'd been so set in our ways and Hillary obviously had different ideas. She used to print out the diary like a little booklet and nobody would ever look at it. We were a bit rebellious really, but actually once we settled into it we realized she took so much pressure off us. It's great now and I love her to bits, don't know what I'd do without her. And Angela, Hillary's number two, is fantastic. She came on board later and so did Lily, our PA. They've grown with us and it's lovely. It's become a friendship and I think that's important. Hillary is just an amazing person, lovely, very loyal. She sees the good in everybody.

NADINE: Before I got in the band I didn't really have any expectations about what it would mean to be a pop star. I just didn't know. I loved the *Divas* TV show and I had this image of Mariah Carey and Whitney Houston on stage singing power ballads and the audience cheering and I thought, that's what it must be like. Then, in 2005, when we did our first tour, 'What Will the Neighbours Say?', it was great. You're up there and the gratification is so instant. To be able to go on stage with what I class as great songs and perform to people who've come just to see us is so good. When we did the 'Greatest Hits' album it was a real buzz to tour that in 2007. If you're putting a tour together you have to think about drops in the show, certain album tracks not all the audience knows that can lull the wow factor, but that tour was buzzing the whole time. It was great to go out and perform. Of course, we then had all the stuff about Girls Aloud splitting. 'If they're doing the greatest hits it must be a farewell tour,' kind of thing.

You have to be in peak physical health to be able to go out and do a show every night and you have to make sure you look after your throat. You just need to eat well, take vitamins – cod liver oil for your joints – drink plenty of water, and make sure you're healthy.

When the tour's coming up it's like you suddenly become really aware of yourself and staying well. The rehearsals get your body ready and then you just have to be careful you don't get any injuries. Our biggest show on the 'Greatest Hits' tour was in Manchester and that morning I banged my leg on the table in my hotel room. I was afraid to look at it; it was cut and swollen, and I was thinking, how am I going to do this show? I was actually fine but I was left with a scar and it still hurts. You get to know little things, dos and don'ts, to make sure you don't get ill, like I've learned I can't wash my hair and go out with it wet in the morning because I did that once before and ended up with a cough.

We're together all the time for weeks, just hanging out and rehearsing, then on the road, and we end up having nothing to talk about. We all watch the same thing on TV just so we can have a conversation about it. I had a whole discussion with Kimberley about a tub of pralines and cream ice cream and how much caramel was in it. That's the kind of stuff that excites you after weeks of rehearsing.

NICOLA: Once I start rehearsing it's really easy for my muscles to bounce back because I used to be a dancer. I'm very lucky, but at the same time I start to lose weight and get skinny and I don't think that's attractive. Literally, a few days in rehearsals and I end up with a six-pack, which I don't like. I don't want my muscles to be slack but there's a difference between wanting to be toned and solid and being skinny. I prefer to be a bit more womanly, so I'm really conscious of eating decent amounts of food. I have to eat every couple of hours anyway because I'm hyperglycaemic but I end up eating more on tour because I know how fast it's being burned off. I've learned the worst thing I can do

is have something sugary, so I try not to leave it to the point where my sugar level starts to plummet and I'm having to eat sweets or drink a Coke or Red Bull or something because I know it's just going to drop again. I have to eat literally an hour before I go on stage, then I run the risk of getting a stitch, but if I didn't eat I'd be performing on empty, so it's quite difficult to manage. I think because your body's full of adrenalin that helps get you through the performance. We all try to eat healthily on tour and do things like have honey and lemon in hot water for our throats, and we take supplements, like Berocca and Echinacea, because when your body's working extra hard you're prone to getting rundown.

KIMBERLEY: Before 'Tangled Up' I was eating really healthily. It's a big deal, a lot of people are coming to see you, so you just want to feel and look the best you can. I was keeping to a low-ish amount of calories, eating things like fish and vegetables, having a piece of chocolate or a few sweets if I wanted them. If you totally deprive yourself of something, you just want it more. I've tried most things over the years – the Atkins Diet, cabbage soup diet, the lot – and they do work for a short period of time, but as soon as you remotely start eating anything nice again the weight comes back on so it's not really worth it, and I wouldn't do anything extreme anyway when I'm dancing.

The dancing gets you toned but we all have days, especially in the first week of rehearsals, where we're worn out. It's like, my God, I can't keep my eyes open. When you get home at night it feels like your muscles are seizing up. I get in a boiling hot bath, which seems to work. I know if I just went to bed I wouldn't be able to walk down the stairs the next day. I went to the chiropractor during the 'Tangled Up' rehearsals and he was like, 'What the hell have you been doing?' My whole left side was completely out of line. I do love the fact you're getting exercise doing something you enjoy. I thrive on it. I want to get fit and get in shape so I go for it full throttle in rehearsal and it does feel good.

NICOLA: We were in the middle of rehearsals for 'Tangled Up' when my little dog, Elvis, died. He was only eight months old and he had a fit. It was such a shock because it wasn't like he'd been ill or anything. I thought maybe he'd had a heart attack but it turned out it he'd caught some disease. The vet said I couldn't have helped him because there weren't any symptoms and we wouldn't have known there was anything wrong. He just seemed fine, a completely healthy puppy, then died just days later.

I was given him on my twenty-second birthday. When I got home after filming *Passions* in Taiwan, there, in the living room, was this tiny puppy in a box. He was so gorgeous, he totally stole my heart. For the few months I had him he was my little saviour. I don't know how I coped with losing him like that and having to go straight back into rehearsals but, to be honest, as much as my heart was broken, and as much as I was devastated, I've been through worse things so I think that's how I was able to handle it. I've had so much stuff in my personal life I just think, 'Why is this happening?' It makes me wonder if losing Elvis was meant to make me stronger because something even worse is going to happen. There's obviously a reason; it has to be fate. If you don't think like that and have faith in things being the way they're meant to be you'd just crack up. I'm still really sad that he's gone, though. I loved him, and this might sound weird but he was like my little best friend and I miss him a lot.

The rehearsals are intense anyway. You get to about a week before the tour starts and you just feel like you can't speak unless you have to, like you can't take any information in. Your head is full, absolutely clogged. Sometimes you find yourself becoming overwhelmed, you feel the pressure. Sometimes you find yourself breaking down for nothing. It's not that you're sad, it's just you need some kind of release because it all gets a bit mad in your head.

You try and stay professional but you have to have a bit of a life at the same time. It's just about making an effort, like booking a table and making sure you're there. It's so easy to come in, put your pyjamas on, sit in front of the telly for two hours, then go to bed, but if you just go out once a week it breaks it up a bit and the conversation the next day isn't all about dancing.

Having someone at home works in two ways because obviously they're waiting for you to get in but then you're absolutely shattered and you can barely string a conversation together so your relationship suffers a little bit, but essentially the other person just needs to understand, take a back seat and be happy for you, because you're doing what you love.

KIMBERLEY: We have four weeks in rehearsal to learn all the routines and put the show together, which doesn't seem like very long, but we always manage it. It's important we know exactly what we're doing and that it's really tight because there are a lot of danger aspects as well.

For the 'Greatest Hits' tour we started the show in a cage that was lowered from the ceiling. It was suspended from wires at each corner and in pre-production at the Nottingham Arena we were all in it for the first time, waiting to be lowered. I don't know exactly how high up it was, but it was a long way down. The music started up, really loud, and the cage started to move but only one side was dropping so it was tipping up on its side. Me and Nicola were at the side that was going down and we thought we were going to fall. She was screaming, petrified, crying, holding on to me.

NICOLA: Every one of us felt vulnerable, just up there, hanging. I thought I was going to go over the edge. Kimberley had hold of me and with the fear and adrenalin our hands were slipping because we were sweating. I was thinking, I am gonna fall to my death. I can be so dramatic!

KIMBERLEY: I was frightened Nicola was going to go and I just had hold of her with one sweaty hand. Eventually the band realized something was wrong and stopped playing and it just felt like everybody was looking at us and didn't know what the hell to do. It was awful. Nobody was saying anything. We were stuck and our hands were slipping. Then they went to move it again and instead of straightening up it went more to the side. By this point we were all screaming. Sarah was in shock, Nadine was crying her eyes out and praying, and Cheryl was trying to stay calm. I was imagining us hanging on and this cage swinging in the air until someone put a crash mat or something underneath it and we all jumped. After what felt like ages they managed to straighten it up and bring us down and as soon as we landed on the floor we all burst out crying. Cheryl had been strong up to that point, going, 'It's fine, it's fine,' but she was in tears with fear and relief. We were all hugging each other, like we'd had a near-death experience. There was that horrible, gut-wrenching fear that it could turn into one of those awful 'TRAGEDY ON TOUR' stories.

NADINE: I remember thinking we were going to die, up there in our stilettos, hanging on. It was awful. Cheryl had a mic and she was so calm, saying we needed help. Down below, the dancers had dispersed and I just had this vision of the cage falling and us plummeting to our death.

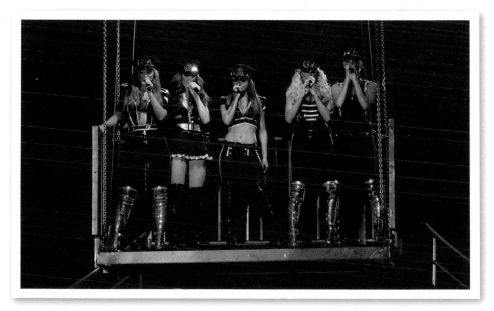

KIMBERLEY: They left it up to us if we wanted to keep that as our entrance for the show – nobody was forcing us – and we decided we still wanted to do it because it was going to look so amazing.

NICOLA: Me and Kimberley switched places so she was at the end but every night it was a massive thing for me to get over at the start of the show. I've got a fear of heights and unless you have that I don't think you understand how frightening it is.

NADINE: People often say once they get on stage the nerves go completely, but that doesn't happen to me. I get nervous for different things at different points. I'll begin a song and do the first part and think, okay, I've got that over, then I'll be thinking about a really high note I've got to hit and I'll get nervous in the lead-up to that. Then I'll find something to be nervous about in the next song, and the next … all the way through the show. When the curtains finally close I'll go phew, it went well. I put so much pressure on myself to do it right and if I don't there's no talking to me.

I had a really bad show in Manchester on the 'Greatest Hits' tour. At the beginning of 'Biology' the crowd was so loud I was just swamped by the noise and couldn't hear so I wasn't quite on pitch and I couldn't get it back. Nobody else even noticed, but I did. It was the last song and I was, like, please, close the curtains quick, and then I just burst out crying. I was screaming and crying I was so disappointed. I think when people are paying to come and see you the least you can do is sing in tune and I didn't for that opening and it bothered me. Cheryl was hugging me and saying, 'Are you okay?' It was the same day I'd hurt my ankle and she thought that's why I was crying, but it was purely because I wasn't happy with the song. Nobody can criticize me as harshly as I do, not when it comes to the job I do. If you call yourself a singer then do a good job and sing in tune.

CHERYL: You can feel the electricity in the arenas. Whatever the crowd's giving you, you're bouncing off it, so if they're a bit flat your performance tends to be a bit flat. You can feel the change in the atmosphere from when you do a sound check in the afternoon and the arena's empty to going on the stage in your outfit with the audience there. It's a totally different feeling.

Before we go on we get together with the boys and Beth and scream and pump each other up. If one person's nervous we all catch it and if one person's hyper, or low, it spreads to everyone. We're all connected so whatever vibes each of us is giving off we all pick up on them. I'm really intuitive as well and I can feel the vibes coming off other people. You just have to know you're there for one another, that whatever happens it's fine. If you hit a bad note, don't worry about it, it's not that big of a deal.

I cried when we played Newcastle in 2008. I hadn't seen any of my family or friends for five months, which is quite an emotional thing anyway. The beauty of this tour was we had a smaller stage in the middle of the arena and all my family were at the front so I could see their faces and my dad and my aunty looked so proud. I could see it in their eyes; it was like, 'That's our Cheryl.'

Geordies are known for being loyal. We love to see one of our own doing well and it was like the whole arena was proud of me. There was a group of teenagers from a cancer trust at the front and they were crying and chanting my name and it was so overwhelming. I couldn't take it. When we went off stage the whole place was chanting, 'Cher-yl, Cher-yl,' and it was really emotional. I felt a bit of an idiot coming off and crying because Geordies are supposed to be made of tough stuff, but I just couldn't hold it in.

When you read letters from fans it puts everything into perspective. In Sheffield, during pre-production for 'Tangled Up', I got a really personal letter from a girl in Newcastle just saying we'd met her the year before and changed her life. That's so powerful.

The fans have always been great in Newcastle but there was a different feeling this year. I don't know how to describe it, just more overwhelming. I felt like I couldn't get my breath. I've never experienced that intensity before; it was so strong. All those people wishing you well is an amazing thing.

NICOLA: We played Liverpool for the first time on the 'Tangled Up' tour. Even though I'm not actually from Liverpool it's the closest I've got to having a home town to perform in and people seem to be proud to feel I'm from there. To be honest, I wasn't sure what kind of a reaction I'd get when we played there, whether it really would feel like home or not, but I got such a good response. And it did feel like home. The crowd, the atmosphere, was just amazing and it was such a good night. When I came off I was so proud. That was my favourite night of the tour.

KIMBERLEY: I always think if you could put a camera on the quick-change backstage it would be funny to see everyone running round, panicking and screaming. We've normally got two minutes, which isn't very long, especially if the costumes have different elements, so the minute you're out of sight something's coming off; your decency goes out the window. It's just a scramble to get back on as quickly as possible and things do sometimes go wrong. On the 'Chemistry' tour, I had this little biker-girl hot-pants suit for the encore and when I went to do the zip up it broke so literally my bra was hanging out and Frank, our wardrobe guy, was trying to stitch me into the costume, but it wasn't how it should be and you just think God, I hope people don't think I'm meant to come out like this. In Sheffield, on the 'Greatest Hits' tour, Nadine was late getting on for one of the sections and we had to buy some time. We ended up improvising for about two minutes of music, just dancing at the top of the stairs, which was so cringe-worthy. The dancers took the initiative and started doing back-flips and stuff. I don't know to what extent the audience were aware of what was going on, but for us it was horrendous.

NADINE: When we were doing the 'Chemistry' tour I got really fed up because I kept asking my family when they were going to come to the show and everyone was, like, 'Oh, we'll see.'

When we got to Newcastle I was moping around thinking no one was going to come and it was awful. I was calling them and nobody was picking up their phone and I was just feeling really depressed.

We did the show and afterwards my friend told me some story about having to come to dinner because her friend was friends with Sting and he'd be there. I really wasn't on form and still no one was answering their phone, but I got dressed and walked into the bar at the hotel and the first thing I saw was my two sisters standing with my mammy. I looked round and there were like 45 people there from Derry and my friend from Dublin and his band playing 'Happy Birthday'. It was a surprise early twenty-first for me. My birthday was a couple of weeks away so I hadn't even been thinking about it and it was just amazing. My face when I saw them all – I was in complete shock. There were balloons everywhere and a cake and an ice sculpture, like a glass slipper. God love them for doing it. That's why nobody would pick up their phone to me all day – they were afraid of putting their foot in it and ruining the surprise.

On my actual twenty-first, on 15 June 2006, we'd done a show in Barcelona and Jesse flew out to meet me. We had dinner that night and late drinks at the bar, then the next day the girls flew back to London, and me and Jesse stayed on. It was the first time either of us had been in Barcelona and we were in a really nice hotel by the marina and just spent the day wandering around, being tourists. It was really sweet, nobody bothering us, just one or two people coming up who knew him off *Desperate Housewives.* Then we flew to Toronto because he had to do some press for *John Tucker Must Die.* The film people had booked us into this really posh restaurant for dinner as a birthday present for me, everyone in tuxedos and ball gowns, all really grown up, and us like two kids. Jesse had a cap on and it was, like, 'Sir, you'll have to remove your cap.' Then we went to LA and he kept telling everyone it was my twenty-first and people were going, 'Oh, that's nice, when's your birthday exactly?' Oh, about a month ago. We kept it going a long time.

KIMBERLEY: I think it was quite hard for my mum and dad when I was little. They'd moved into a nice house in a suburb of Bradford and then my dad's business went bust and that had a dramatic effect on things. They really wanted to stay in the house because we were happy and settled there, but it was a struggle to keep things going. There were four of us: my older sister, Sally, me, my brother, Adam, and my little sister, Amy. When she was born things were quite hard, money-wise, by then. I'd have been nearly five and Amy was just a baby when Mum and Dad got divorced. We stayed in the house with my mum, but it wasn't easy. She worked full-time as a teacher, did piano lessons after school, made clothes to sell, did parties where people came round – any way she could make extra money – and that's how we survived. She had so much to deal with: going through a divorce, trying to keep the house, feed and clothe four children – a baby, a two-year-old, a four-year-old and a six-year-old. I think it was a tough time for my mum. She wasn't able to hold it together all the time and I do remember seeing her upset, a lot, and it was hard. As kids, we were totally aware things were difficult; we knew exactly what was going on.

There'd been a lot of arguing up to the point when my dad went, and even at that young age you know it's better if he goes because then there won't be any more arguments. Even though they'd split we still saw him all the time. He'd come and take us to school every day and aside from it being hard not living with him any more, we got to spend quality time with him. It would have been difficult if they'd both got with long-term partners straight away, but they didn't, so we felt we were still at the centre of both their worlds. I've always been close to both my parents. Then we all started saying we wanted to go to stage school. God knows how Mum managed it. She did everything for us and I don't think I heard her moan once. She's just one of those women, a real inspiration. What we saw her go through, it really makes you respect your mum, and we just felt we were all in it together. We didn't want to be bad at school or do anything to give her any more hurt and I think that's why we're all really close still. She did an amazing job.

FULL NAME
Kimberley Jane

BORN
20 November 1981, in
Bradford, West Yorkshire

STYLE
Laid-back, secure, grounded

INTO
Performing, touring, cooking

CAN'T STAND
The pressure on women to be
a certain size/shape

SHE SAYS
'The music industry is a
dangerous place to be if
you're not a secure person.'

213

I wasn't remotely shy as a child. I come from a musical family – Dad was in a band, Mum's a music teacher and plays the piano, guitar and clarinet, and they can both sing – so I can see where I got it from. I'd get up and sing for anyone, any time. All of us were into performing. My older sister's an actress, my brother does modelling and stuff, and my younger sister's at drama school. Mum would take us to stage school in an old church hall in Bradford and I'd just always be singing and dancing. We were doing shows at the Alhambra, which is a really gorgeous theatre in Bradford, and I got quite a few solo parts, which you'd think would have stood me in good stead for *Popstars: The Rivals*, but I don't think anything could have prepared me for that. I think my parents probably had to sacrifice a lot but they always encouraged us and my poor mum did those journeys to stage school every night. We were really lucky because not every family would be prepared to do that – drive their kids to auditions, or to speech and drama festivals and dance competitions – but we had some brilliant opportunities over the years. It was my dad who'd take us to auditions and stuff because he was working in sales and could get a couple of hours off, whereas my mum's a teacher. I think he instilled it in me to get to places on time because we were always early, then we'd sit in a café and we'd go through the script together before I went in to audition. He was always really involved.

I was a real chatterbox at school and sometimes I'd get in trouble for singing while I was working and I honestly didn't realize I was doing it. I wouldn't say I was a brilliant student, but I wasn't bad either. I could have put a lot more effort in but I got by and I'd always do a bit extra around the time of exams, do it all at the last minute, and it kind of worked for me.

I was always working when I was young. I got a job cleaning a bakery from top to bottom when I was 13. I'm a bit of a clean freak so it was all right, but it was pretty hard labour at that age for the £10 I got. I did ironing as well for a woman who lived up the road and got a tenner for that, then when I was a bit older me and a friend worked in a bakery in Ilkley at the weekend, then I got a job in a diner and a tapas restaurant. Sometimes I'd work both weekend days and both nights and I vividly remember my mum begging me to take a night off, but I quite enjoyed working.

I landed a part in a TV series called *The Booktower* when I was five and that kind of got me in with ITV, so I'd do voiceovers and stuff and I was always up for different things. When I was 11, I was on my way to audition for *Les Misérables* in Manchester when the car hit black ice, spun round, careered off the road and hit a wall. My aunty was driving and my sister and cousin were in the car with us. I've no idea how no one was hurt because all these boulders had flown through the windows. There were lumps of rock in the car around us but somehow they'd missed everybody. We were all shaken up but I was still determined to go for my audition. I got there an hour and a half late, walked on stage, sang, and got the part. I'm really glad I didn't wimp out because that experience gave me the bug and made me realize I wanted to sing for a job. It wasn't like I just woke up one day and thought I'd be a pop star; it was a lifelong ambition and I worked so hard for it – training, doing anything and everything I could to get where I am. Sometimes people don't see that; they assume you turned up for an audition one day and it's that easy, but it's never like that. Most people who get somewhere have always wanted to do it and have a history of trying all sorts to get there.

Q What makes you cry?

A I get a bit upset sometimes when my mum comes to see me and then goes back to Bradford because it never seems like she's here long enough. She came down for Mother's Day and I got a bit teary because I hadn't seen her for a while.

Q Have you had any hair disasters?

A I had a terrible perm when I was 13/14. Everybody had curly hair and mine was dead straight and fine so I had it permed and I looked like a poodle. There was this big sprout of hair at the front that looked awful. I used to do my own highlights when I was a teenager and a couple of times it went grey and silver and an awful yellowy colour.

Q Do you lose your temper?

A I do, but not that much. I don't ever lose my temper with my family or friends because I don't see enough of them to waste time arguing.

Q What's in your bag on a night out?

A My phone, a credit card and some cash, keys, chewing gum. I always take lip gloss and sometimes eyeliner and a bit of powder because I think I'll reapply it, but as soon as I'm enjoying myself it's the last thing I can be bothered to do.

Q What do you enjoy cooking?

A I'm not brilliant at throwing things together. I prefer to cook from recipes. I do a few Jamie Oliver and Nigella things: fish dishes, risotto, ravioli, that kind of stuff. I'm getting into Caribbean food because Justin's dad makes it, so I've made salt fish fritters and king prawns in jerk seasoning. Banana cake is a weakness. I've been making it for years. I took one to Cheryl's once and Ashley ate half of it in two minutes, so now she makes it as well. On tour, me and Sarah had a bake-off, which is really sad and not what pop stars should do; I made buns and she did flapjacks.

Q Have you met any inspiring celebrities?

A Alicia Keys really inspired me. She's so talented, so normal and lovely, just loves her job and gets on with it. Denzel Washington was unbelievable. I nearly died when I found out we were going to meet him. I was watching Jonathan Ross the week before we were going to be on and he said, 'Next week, Girls Aloud, Denzel Washington …' I was running round the house, my heart going, because he's been my favourite actor for years. He was just a genuinely nice person, and so friendly. I was desperate to ask for a picture but I didn't want to embarrass him. I wish I had now.

Q Do you count your blessings?

A Yeah, I do, quite regularly. It could all go away just like that. You can get wrapped up in things and this is quite an unnatural position to be in at this age, to be so financially secure … it's not normal. It's not what everybody has. If you're aware of what you have and appreciate it, hopefully you'll have more chance of keeping hold of it.

cover
GIRLS

Think Girls Aloud, think glamour. They each have their own individual sense of style and beauty, and a unique take on being pop pin-ups. When it comes to looking good and staying in shape the girls know what works for them, and what doesn't. Get their low-down on food, fashion, stress, skin-care, sunburn, cellulite, colonics, weight, (not) working-out, health-kicks, high heels, going out in their pyjamas – and more.

NADINE: I'm not into working out. I hate sweating and running and getting that red-faced look. I've got this thing called a Fluidity Bar which is a mixture of Pilates and yoga done on a ballet barre. It's low-impact, very feminine, just small movements, and I've been doing that in LA. The outfits we wear on tour don't leave much to the imagination so you want to be in the best shape you can. Weight is very simple for me. I'll eat a whole tub of ice cream if I want it but if I see it on myself in a couple of days then that's it, no more. I'll ease off the chocolate and whatever until my clothes fit again. If I was that bothered about my weight I'd do sit-ups and work out but I can't be, because I don't.

I always drink water because you just know it's good for you and I've always liked healthy food. Even as a kid I liked fruit and vegetables. I preferred sliced cucumber to sweets and I was never really much of a meat eater. My niece is like me. I went into the house the other night and she was sitting down with a bowl of chopped-up lettuce. Just chopped-up lettuce. I do love mashed potatoes – that's my favourite. Now and then I binge a bit on junk food. It'll not cross my mind to have any for ages then I'll want loads all at once. I'll eat it until it makes me sick then I'll be off it for ages until I'm in the mood again.

I have a really good set of beauty products that I cannot stray from. I use Origins, which are naturally made and really work for me. I'm obsessed with moisturizers, especially when I'm travelling,

> *I don't really do much pampering stuff. After a tour when you've been wearing loads of make-up and sweating I might get a really good facial but it's not a routine thing. I think when you're obsessed with how you look you can't have that much else to worry about.*

because you dry out on the plane, but for ages I couldn't find a good one. I tried them all, from the really expensive ones to the cheap ones, and they all clogged up my pores and gave me bad skin. I don't like putting anything oily on my face and the Origins oil-free moisturizer works. The others girls don't use it and sometimes Liz, our make-up artist, will try to sneakily put something else on my face and I'm, like, 'No!' I know I'll end up having spots. I don't really do much pampering stuff. After a tour when you've been wearing loads of make-up and sweating I might get a really good facial but it's not a routine thing. I think when you're obsessed with how you look you can't have that much else to worry about.

KIMBERLEY: I don't have a strict beauty routine. I've always been lucky and had all right skin and I just make sure I clean it really well and use plenty of moisturizer. I don't do anything out of the ordinary and I'm not one to buy into lotions and potions. I just stick to simple things. I'll have a facial now and then, just for the pleasure of it, but if my skin's all right I'll leave it.

In terms of clothes, I think I have a certain style and I cater to my own shape, which I think is a good tip for everybody. I tend to be more covered up than some people you see out and about but that's my choice. I'd say that if part of your outfit's going to be revealing keep the rest a bit covered up so you look classy; never have your stomach out and your legs and your boobs.

I love dresses and they're everywhere now. You can get so many different shapes and fabrics and patterns and waistlines. You know if you've got a dress that fits well you don't have to worry about

matching different things to make an outfit; it just simplifies everything. A good tip is if you feel comfortable in something it probably looks good.

I love fashion and I like to put outfits together, but it doesn't matter in the slightest to me if something cost £20 or £2,000. I'm just not a label girl, and personally I can't spend huge amounts of money on things. I would lose sleep over it. I think £600 for a handbag is a lot and I can't really do it. I don't think you need to spend money like that when there are so many nice things around that are affordable. I still shop at Topshop and I'll go on net-a-porter.com for slightly more designer things, but I'd never spend £1,000 on an item – never. I don't even look at things over a certain price. I do most of my shopping online because it takes the stress away, especially if I'm working hard and don't have much time. Topshop.com is good and aldoshoes.com is reasonable and really nice. I even shop for make-up at maccosmetics.co.uk. I used to go shopping on my own but I don't like doing that any more. I've ended up surrounded by loads of young lads and it's quite overwhelming. You do feel a bit out of your depth.

NICOLA: My style is changing all the time and I'm really growing and loving the fact that I look more individual than anybody else, and I like to dress to suit that. For ages I didn't know what my style was but now I take a real pride in what I wear. I think style is a form of expression and your personality is reflected in how outgoing your style is, how far you're prepared to push it. I will try most looks and I'm not afraid to wear different trends. I love experimenting with clothes. I wear more dresses now, more skirts. Before, I hated the colour of my legs so I'd never put a dress on without thinking I had to put fake tan on and then I'd end up putting on trousers or jeans instead, but I don't have that problem any more. I don't feel paranoid if my legs are white. A great find for me is a product that's like a shine reflector by MAC, which I put on my legs instead of fake tan so they don't look blue-white, just glossy. It's like a pearl effect and it gives a nice sheen to your skin.

I think when you're a young girl you need guidance from other people and I've looked at women like Sophie Ellis-Bextor and Lily Cole and I love how individual they are. Sophie Ellis-Bextor, especially, has such an iconic look; I just think she's flawless.

I hate to wear tracksuits and trainers now. I feel a mess, an absolute slob. In the early days when we were all living in the same block in north London I remember going round to the local shop one night with Kimberley and Cheryl. I'd just got out of the shower, my hair was wet and it had arranged itself into a middle parting, I'd put on fake tan so I was glowing and sticky, and I had no make-up on. I was wearing my pyjama bottoms and an old hoodie. Cheryl and Kimberley were in their pyjamas as well and the people in the shop were staring and whispering. They were like, 'Is that Girls Aloud?' Kimberley just said, 'I think we'd better go back to the car . . .' I won't leave the house now without a pair of heels. I just feel more elegant and I can walk better in heels than flat soles. It's weird, I feel like a woman when I've got my heels on, and as soon as I take them off I feel like a little girl again.

SARAH: I was a comfortable size 10/12 when I got in the band, a naturally curvy D cup, and now there's nothing left, but I'm happier the size I am. People say TV adds 10 pounds and it's only when I look back at all our pictures at the beginning I can see we looked chubby, but we weren't. I had love handles and a bit of a pot belly but I always had a six-pack underneath. I was a nice curvy girl and I didn't pay attention to any of that until I got in the band, then every aspect of your appearance is scrutinized and you look back and think wow, what a difference. I think that's why people in this business can get a complex about their weight.

I'm a real foodie, despite what people say about us not eating, but maybe it's anxiety that keeps the weight off. Stress and everything and working off nervous energy has probably a lot to do with it. I like going to the gym and I go through phases when I do a lot of working out and I'm either very healthy – or not healthy at all. My last flat had a gym in the complex so I could just walk over, do all the cardio, a few weights, stretches, sit-ups, sit in the sauna until I'd melted, then jump in the pool and do 50 lengths. All or nothing. I think a lot of the time running round right, left and centre, dancing, doing rehearsals with the girls – all that helps you keep in shape. When we're touring we have a good month of dancing every day, rehearsing, learning routines, and I tone up with all that.

If I'm on a health kick I'll juice, not to lose weight, just to pump myself full of healthy stuff, and I'll make a big green smoothie with celery, cucumber, spinach, avocado, pineapple and supplements – Spirulina, digestive enzymes, all that Gillian McKeith stuff – blend it up with ice and take it with me in a flask every day.

I did a detox at a clinic in Austria in 2007, just for a week, for a good old spring clean to feel healthy again. I did the whole shebang – colonics, daily lymphatic massage, blood tests. It was like a cross between a hospital and a hotel. The only proper meal was at lunchtime. I was on water and herbal tea, sheep's milk cheese on rice crackers, maybe an egg or a piece of ham. For dinner I'd have rice crackers and herbal tea, and that was it. Some nights I was so hungry I couldn't sleep – my stomach would be growling at me. I went with my friend Steve [Lyall]. He wanted to quit smoking and every day we'd be, like, 'Oh my God, are you starving?' 'Yes – are you?' 'Yes!'

You had to take Epsom salts in the morning before breakfast to clean you out, and have clay shakes, which are disgusting. At night I'd have a liver wrap – a hot water bottle wrapped in a cold towel that they put against your liver – to draw out impurities. Some days I felt like death, all the toxins coming out, bags under my eyes, spotty, and I'd be saying I can't do this any more. Then the next day I'd feel great, full of the joys of spring.

> ❛ By the end of the week I had to have chocolate. This was February, so it was really cold, and me and Steve cycled 15 kilometres round this lake in Austria to find a shop. ❜

By the end of the week I had to have chocolate. This was February, so it was really cold, and me and Steve cycled 15 kilometres round this lake in Austria to find a shop. It was Sunday and there was hardly anywhere open. We'd only taken five euros so we didn't go mad and ruin everything, and we found a patisserie, bought something, and it wasn't very nice. I ended up going into a doughnut shop with almost no money and just about begging for something. They were like, 'Oh, you must be from the clinic …' There must be a few people who escape and try to get something decent inside them.

When I got back home I'd lost some weight and was just a lot healthier. I felt great. I'd discovered that my food intolerances are gluten and fructose. I can't have anything with fruit sugar and I've noticed that if I have too much wheat I do suffer quite badly and get bloated, but it's impossible to cut those out completely. It does wonders if you stick to it but realistically, with our lifestyles, sometimes you're just going to have to take what food's given. I try to keep it healthy, everything in moderation, but I still get the odd craving for a McDonald's.

I am one for trying loads of remedies, a sucker for a gimmick, anything that comes up on TV. 'Oh, the tummy toner – let's try one!' I'm always trying new supplements. On tour, I'm like a walking medicine bag. We'll be in the car and one of the girls will go, 'Look, Sarah, it's your favourite hang-out,' and, no, it's not the Hawley Arms – it'll be a pharmacy.

NADINE: I always had a major issue with my legs; they're just too skinny and I have never liked them. I was convinced trousers looked much better than skirts on me, especially when performing, but TV adds weight so it makes my legs look a normal size. The first time I wore a skirt on TV was the night we found out we'd got to number one with 'Sound of the Underground'. The stylist just said, 'You're wearing a skirt, I don't care what you say, I'm not getting you any trousers.' I was like, okay, and that was it. I didn't have one pair of trousers in the entire Girls Aloud wardrobe for ages. It's funny, I would still be like that about my legs. I'd look at them sometimes and want to throw up. They're like toothpicks. I don't have that same hang-up about them now, but I still don't think they're great.

NICOLA: I've got really sensitive skin so anything too perfumed or harsh makes it break out. I use Garnier at the moment and I just keep things really simple. I wash my face and that's it. Too much washing, exfoliating, facial wipes, all that, aggravates it. I went through a stage of really scrubbing my skin and it just made it worse. I realized I need to leave it alone. I wash it in the morning and wash my make-up off

> ❛ I don't bother with expensive products because to be honest, after going to Taiwan with *Passions* and seeing how things are made, it's the label and the packaging you're paying for. ❜

before bed and that's really all it needs. I use moisturizer, a bit of eye cream and lip balm and that's it. I don't bother with expensive products because to be honest, after going to Taiwan with *Passions* and seeing how things are made, it's the label and the packaging you're paying for.

When I'm stressed it really affects my body. I lose weight and get bad skin. This year, for the first time ever, I took antibiotics for my skin because I thought it was looking terrible. I'm working on trying not to get stressed or worry about things. I feel like even when my mind's working overtime my body is losing weight. My mum's the same.

I don't really bother with pampering but I do like doing girly things, like having a pedicure and my nails done, and just being well groomed. I have my eyelashes and eyebrows tinted because they're completely blonde so when I've got no make-up on it looks like I've got no eyes, and I couldn't live without my Dainty Doll foundation and concealer. It's an absolute lifesaver for my skin colour. Now I have an exact skin colour foundation and short hair, I'm less maintenance!

SARAH: I've always been an extrovert, but when I was younger I was so insecure I wouldn't go to school without putting on a full face of make-up about an inch thick. I was always being sent home or getting detention for having too much make-up on. I was just so embarrassed if I had a spot. I was really shy. I'm not like that now, but I've only really started coming out of my shell as I've got older. The only time I felt confident when I was younger was when I was on a stage. Being in the band has helped me be a more confident, outspoken person away from the stage as well. I'm much happier in my own skin now.

CHERYL: I do try to make the best of myself and work out and keep healthy, but I don't take it too seriously. I've been using the same L'Oréal face wash for the past five years and I just make sure my face is clean and that I'm cleansed and moisturized before I go to bed. Other than that, I haven't got any secrets. I don't want to be perfect, don't want to have that pressure to constantly look pristine and then one day I'm not and it's like, 'Oh my God, look at the state of Cheryl.' I still nip to the garage in my pyjamas for a pint of milk.

❛ The morning I was number two in *FHM*'s 100 Sexiest Women in the World somebody called to tell me and I was half asleep. I looked in the mirror and just laughed because I thought, if you could see me now . . . I mean, who wouldn't look good with their hair done by a top stylist, face made up by a professional make-up artist and dressed to the nines? ❜

I've got a Hypoxi-therapy bike for cellulite, for bum, hips and thighs. It's like a pod and you sit in it and as you're pedalling it kind of pops the fat cells, which I love, of course.

I'm so flattered to have nice things said about me but I do find it hilarious when I'm in men's magazines and I read that people think I'm gorgeous or whatever. The morning I was number two in *FHM*'s 100 Sexiest Women in the World [2005] somebody called to tell me and I was half asleep. I looked in the mirror and just laughed because I thought, if you could see me now . . . I mean, who wouldn't look good with their hair done by a top stylist, face made up by a professional make-up artist and dressed to the nines? I find it quite funny that people think of me like that. All the sex-symbol stuff, I just have to laugh. I often feel sorry for Ashley. I'll be in one of his big, baggy jumpers, no make-up on, hair tied up in a bobble, eyebrows skew-whiff, bags under my eyes, in a pair of terrible slippers I've had for five years and I'm, like, 'These people think I'm sexy! You should take a picture and send it to them.'

NICOLA: My skin is so fragile I just don't cope in the sun. I burn very easily and I have to be careful because my scalp fries and that's painful. A few years ago I'd gone to Majorca and I fell asleep in the sun and just got absolutely frazzled. It was so bad I was saying I needed to go to the hospital. The skin on my chest was actually cut. I got back to the room and I could hardly move; all my skin had tightened. I couldn't even rub after-sun into it, it was so sore. The pain was unreal. I didn't sleep a wink, just lay crying all night. I'd been burned before but never like that, my whole body. The next day I went down to the pool, wrapped myself in soaking towels from head to toe, and lay under a brolly. I remember these two women walking past in their swimming costumes, all bronzed and golden, and there was me lying there, cocooned in towels, my eyes bright red from being burned. It was really bad.

A few weeks later my skin must still have been tender because we shot the 'Love Machine' video and I had this blue dress on with tit-tape to keep it up, and when I took it off it ripped my skin. From then on I just thought, this is really dangerous, I could seriously damage myself, so now I don't even try to catch the sun. It's not worth it. I use P20, which is really good and just blocks it off. They say you only need to put it on once but I put it on three or four times a day just to be sure. It's funny, I used to be always putting fake tan on and now I wouldn't like to tan. You just grow used to who you are.

CHERYL: People have this false idea that we have a machine around us that drives us, and of course when we have a full diary we have a stylist because we have to look consistent as a band, but sometimes I'll go out and it'll be, 'Sack the stylist!' Do they really think I got a stylist over or a make-up artist round to my house just to go out to a club? No. I'm a normal girl and I put on whatever I choose to wear. People have this idea everything's controlled, and it's not.

I think your style changes anyway as you get older. I used to be a bit tomboyish and loved trainers and Timberland boots and baggy trousers, so when I got in the band that's what I wanted. I wanted to dance in trainers. I used to be a ballerina and I've got sore feet anyway, so I used to struggle in heels sometimes on video shoots, like be in tears it was so painful, but I've become more accustomed to them now.

I had to have an operation on my feet in 2007 because I'd had a lot of problems from doing ballet. They broke three of my toes and straightened them with metal pins and I was laid up for two months. It was horrendous. I scratched my stitches, just forgot about them and . . . oh my God, that memory haunts me. And the needle they put in the back of your hand when you have an operation, I can't bear the feeling of it. When I went to get the pins out I said I didn't want that but it was there when I woke up. I pulled it out myself and the nurse went mad but I had to, just had to get it out; it was making me feel sick.

NICOLA: When it comes to cosmetic surgery most of me thinks, you know what, be proud to be the woman you are, but I think that comes with age and wisdom. I'm lucky that there's no part of me that makes me really unhappy, but I do know people who aren't in that situation and will be unhappy about something forever. You only have one life to live, so why not be happy? People having lots of procedures, that's an addiction, and it's a problem but I think, in general, it's a personal preference. I think we live in a society that's very judgemental and people feel the pressure to look good. Everybody wants to be accepted, everybody wants to look pretty. The truth is no one's perfect, but if something's making you really unhappy, fine, get it done. Who's to judge?

CHERYL: I just think if it's not broke don't fix it, basically. People don't even know the consequences of Botox yet; it hasn't been around long enough for people to know what's going to happen to their face in 20 years' time. I'm terrified of needles anyway but the thought of doing it for vanity – no way. When I'm hearing that 16-year-old girls are getting boob jobs, it's worrying. Your body's not finished developing – my body's still changing now and I'm 25 – so messing round with your body at 16, 17, is really frightening. I can understand women that have had four kids and used to have a nice pair of boobs, yes, maybe, if you're that unhappy, but for me personally I just think it's terrifying.

There's loads of things you wish you could change, but I went through all that in my late teens: I hate that, I hate this. I got to a point where I thought, actually I like that, I don't like that, I don't mind that, and rather than dwelling on the negatives I just thought, nobody's perfect, nobody's ever going to be, so I'll focus on the stuff I like instead of the stuff I don't like. I tried loads to change the shape of my legs, all these different exercises, machines and Pilates, and it wasn't doing anything so I just had to get to the point of thinking these are my legs, at least I can walk, be grateful for that. As a woman you're never going to be 100 per cent satisfied with how you are anyway – you'll always want something you haven't got – so I'm just grateful for the good things.

We're all individuals and the quirky things make a character. You normally find it's the imperfections and insecurities that attract you to someone. It would be so intimidating to be faced with the perfect person, just awful. People go on about the bump in my nose but I don't mind it. It's character. I wouldn't mess around with my face. If a surgeon messes your face up you're screwed. I discovered that in this industry you come across a lot of 'done' faces and you think, 'Actually, she looked better before because she was unique.' You can make a doll, can't you? You could make yourself perfect but then you wouldn't be you.

NICOLA

FAVE PRODUCTS
Dainty Doll foundation and concealer, eyelash curlers, MAC shine cream.

COULDN'T LIVE WITHOUT
Face wipes, a regular eyelash tint.

TOP TIP
Go for make-up that suits you, not what you want to look like. Do your make-up in natural light if you can. Vaseline on your eyelashes at night makes them grow. Cheek shader gives your face structure.

SARAH

FAVE PRODUCTS
I love the Estée Lauder facial range and Johnson's PH5.5 face wash. I wear different make-up brands but love L'Oréal mascara and Eylure false eyelashes.

COULDN'T LIVE WITHOUT
Lip gloss, eyelash curlers.

TOP TIP
If you're looking tired, put concealer under your eyes and bronzer on your cheeks – or wear a big hat!

NADINE

FAVE PRODUCTS
Origins skin care, Vaseline on lips,
L'Oréal Shocking Volume mascara.

COULDN'T LIVE WITHOUT
Tweezers, baby wipes.

TOP TIP
Less is more. Use mascara and blusher
and that's the basics sorted.

KIMBERLEY

FAVE PRODUCTS
I love MAC and L'Oréal skin care.
I also use cold cream from Boots.

COULDN'T LIVE WITHOUT
Mascara and lip gloss.

TOP TIP
Practice makes perfect, so experiment
with different make-up at home.

CHERYL

FAVE PRODUCTS
L'Oréal Pure Zone Step 1 – great for
exfoliating. MAC face and body
foundation is really natural. L'Oréal
Shocking Volume mascara.

COULDN'T LIVE WITHOUT
Elizabeth Arden 8-Hour Cream.

TOP TIP
If you only have time to do one thing,
make it mascara, as it makes your eyes
look more awake.

GIRLS
with attitude

'The new queens of the block are Girls Aloud … When you hear them it's as if pop has been created from scratch all over again, this time perfectly.' Julie Burchill, the *Guardian*.

Six years on, Girls Aloud are the queens of UK pop. The *Observer* declared their 2005 release, 'Biology', the single of the decade. In 2007, the *Guinness World Records* immortalised them as the 'Most Successful Reality TV Group'. The *Guardian* featured *The Sound of Girls Aloud: Greatest Hits* in its 2007 list of '1,000 albums to hear before you die'. As well as making ground-breaking pop, they've turned their hands to songwriting, presenting, modelling, acting … and more.

CHERYL: I really believe we were meant to be together and the success we've had proves it. Bands like us don't usually stick around this long or get in the *Guinness Book of Records* for having 18 consecutive top-10 hits, so we've achieved much more than we ever anticipated. We've had quite out-there music and have been fortunate to work with a fantastic team and we've definitely accomplished more than a lot of bands. We never had any kind of game plan. In fact, being naïve and inexperienced in the industry was a kind of a plus to start off with because we learned along the way. We weren't groomed to perfection and we were allowed to do and say what we wanted. It was never my motivation to get to a sixth album or anything; it was just to do what I love doing, which is performing. I saw some TV programme recently where people in the industry were calling us a well-oiled machine and it's so not the case. It was always just us being us.

Everything has had that I-can't-believe-we've-done-that feeling, from being on *Top of the Pops* to getting nominated at the Brits. When we were at the Brits in 2005 it was exciting but we kind of felt we didn't belong. We were in the category for Best Pop Act [with Avril Lavigne, Natasha Bedingfield, Westlife and McFly]

and lost out to McFly and it was like people were looking at us as if to say we didn't deserve to be there – which they probably weren't, but that's how it felt. In 2008 it felt different. I just thought, you know what, I'm going to smile and enjoy the night because we're up for the best gong – Best British Group – we're the only girls in the category, and I'm proud to be here. Winning a Brit is the one thing I would love us to do as a band. You couldn't get more British than us and to be recognized by your own and have that award to show your children is a big deal.

SARAH: The one thing we all aspire to is winning a Brit. We were nominated for Best British Group in 2008 [with the Editors, Kaiser Chiefs, Take That and Arctic Monkeys] and if we'd won it would have been the icing on the cake. That would have been idyllic, but we lost out to the Arctic Monkeys. It did feel a lot different being at the Brits this time. We've had some really good, credible songs along the way, an eclectic bunch of singles and albums, and I think we've earned our place. We've outlived the likes of Busted so we've proved ourselves. The thing about the Brits is that it sometimes feels like they fill the show with American artists and there's less support for the British acts. It's difficult as a girl band to be accepted and seen as credible, but I think we are now – although sometimes it's like we're a bit of a guilty secret, and people won't openly admit they like us. Pop's evolved, become a bit edgier, and we're not a typical pop band so maybe it's hard to find a category for the likes of us, yet a few years back, in 2000, the Spice Girls were up there getting an award for outstanding contribution.

NICOLA: I was so excited to go to the Brits in 2008. We had to get a flight back from Los Angeles and go straight there from the airport, and I was terrified in case the flight was delayed or cancelled. I was so proud we had been nominated. On the night we met Paul McCartney when he got his Outstanding Contribution to Music Award. He'd just come off stage after doing five big numbers and I was thinking, he won't want to meet anyone, he'll need a bit of time to come down after performing, get back on Planet Earth, but not at all. We went to his dressing room and he was like, 'Come in girls!' He was so charismatic and cool, so easy-going, having his photo taken, a real gentleman. He looked amazing too. He's my mum's idol and I was texting her saying, 'You're never going to believe this …' She was like, 'Don't tell me, I'm too jealous.' He's a real inspiration. I remember walking away and thinking, 'Wow.' Sometimes you meet people and they're not what you thought they'd be but he was so nice, so much more than I expected.

CHERYL: I'm doing *The X Factor* and I find it strange that I was once on that spot auditioning and now I'm behind the table with the judges. I actually hate to think I'm judging people; it's more about passing comment, giving my opinion. I met Simon [Cowell] when I did *The Apprentice* for Comic Relief in 2007 and we just clicked. That's when he decided he would like to work with me because he liked my passion. He asked me to be a judge on *Britain's Got Talent* but it just wasn't the right time. A lot's happened since then; Girls Aloud have done a massive tour, we've had more hits, I've done more TV, I did 'Heartbreaker', the single with Will.i.am in 2008, so I feel ready now for *The X Factor*.

It was scary on my first day, but I was more scared of the environment than what I was expected to do. Once I'd settled in and knew I could just be me it was fine. It's more scary sitting next to Louis Walsh …! It was surreal because he judged me all those years ago and I think he was a bit uncomfortable to start with. He came straight into the dressing room and was probably the most welcoming out of everybody. I think maybe he feels a little bit guilty about Girls Aloud.

> Obviously, the judges have their differences of opinion, but what's the point of being there if they don't?

He's admitted he can't work with girls and that's okay. You can't argue with what he's achieved with Westlife and Boyzone. I don't hold grudges; what's the point? It just eats you up. Louis isn't bothered, so me stewing over things he did or didn't do years ago isn't going to help. Anyway, the show's not about us; it's about the people singing for their lives.

I don't blame Louis for anything. He actually did us the biggest favour by keeping away and not being hands-on, because we had to learn for ourselves as a band and that was good for us. I love the journey we've been on and Louis not being involved is a big part of that, so there's nothing to be bitter about. We actually get on. He's all right. He makes me laugh and he's not malicious or anything.

Obviously, the judges have their differences of opinion, but what's the point of being there if they don't? There's no 'beef' with Dannii, despite what the papers say. I'm actually quite sensitive and not catty and I happen to think that women of Dannii's age are at their most confident, sexy and attractive. By then you've shaken off the stuff you've been through, you know what suits you hair- and clothes-wise, you're stronger from experience and I think that's when women are at their most gorgeous. Stuff in the papers about me being this new young model coming in is really embarrassing. I'm uncomfortable with it because I don't feel like that at all.

A lot of people think Simon is harsh and nasty, but he's not, not one bit. He's got a heart of gold. He's real, very charismatic, and he's a pleasure to work with. He's always got time for people. It's amazing to watch him because he'll always acknowledge people around him; even if he's got four TV shows going on he's got time for people, he's always smiling, and a really good energy to be around. He makes me feel really comfortable. He gets Northerners, the Northern mentality. I find a lot of people down south, if they've been brought up in quite a privileged way, public school or whatever, they're quite far removed from what I am because I'm from a council estate in Newcastle, went to the most normal school, and that's worlds apart from Simon, and yet he gets me, gets my humour. I find it really intriguing.

I have a big problem with the 14-year-old category because knowing what we went through as a band it's too much pressure for someone that age. You can't be a role model for thousands of kids when you're a kid yourself. I think you should be a kid while you can. This is an adults' world so just have your youth and forget the pressure. When you're 14–20, those are the most vulnerable years in anyone's life, regardless of whether you're a pop star, so to have the added pressure of magazines scrutinizing you – I just don't agree with it, and I don't like having to have an opinion on someone so young. Look at the history of child stars; the statistics are not good. It messes you up. I hate being put in a position where I even have to pass comment. If I say yes I'm contradicting myself because I think they're too young, and if I say no I'm crushing their dreams. If they're talented at 14 what's the harm in coming back in two years' time? I wanted it when I was 14 but I'm so glad I didn't get it then because by the time I got into Girls Aloud I had more life experience, I knew what I wanted – that I wanted to be in a band, not solo. So that's the hardest, but that's just my opinion.

Out of all the judges, I've been there and I've succeeded. I feel I can empathize with people because I've stood on that spot and I can say

if I feel people don't have what it takes to cut it in the industry, that they're too nervous or whatever.

I'm really glad to be doing *The X Factor* because I hope people will get a chance to see a different side of me. I think the media creates a perception, almost a caricature, and some people play up to that, but I refuse to. They've created this aggressive, gobby character, and I'm nothing like that. I went through a stage where I'd read something and think – am I like that? I actually went through a big identity crisis. I was thinking – do I offend people? Do I make catty comments without realizing? Now I'm more comfortable with myself and having the girls was my sanity. I was able to ask them – did I really say that in that way? Was I out of order? And they'd say no. I think if I'd been a solo artist I'd have gone crackers.

No matter what happens we'll be eternally proud of what we've achieved. None of us are complacent and nobody's under the illusion that anything lasts forever. We're all getting a bit older now and some of us are going to want to start having families one day and settling down. We all know that at some point there'll be a break, it's inevitable. I sometimes think about what I might be doing a few years down the line and I'm just grateful there are so many opportunities, so many things I want to try. I've been offered movie scripts, but at the time it wasn't right, I wasn't ready, and my priority is Girls Aloud. Every decision I make I take the other four girls into consideration. We've been on this journey together and I wouldn't want to do anything that would risk their careers. I'm one of those people, no matter what I do I have to give it my all, so I always want to be challenged in life. I love that feeling of achievement and the whole thing of not having to depend on anyone else and that would always keep me working and striving.

I loved doing the TV series, *Passions*, which aired on ITV2 in March 2008. Sarah, Kimberley and Nicola also did the series. It was a chance to make a film about something each of us was really passionate about and I chose street dancing. I took it and ran with it and thoroughly enjoyed it. I'd seen the David LaChapelle film *Rize*, about kids in LA and this kind of aggressive street dance called 'krumping'. These kids have nothing. There's so much violence and racism in the neighbourhood, gangs and stuff, and instead of using guns or knives their form of battling each other is dance. I loved every minute of doing *Passions*. It's one of the best things I've ever experienced in my life, meeting those kids and Tommy the Clown. It was a real inspiration. I admire them so much. I don't see any reason why we can't do things like that as long as everyone's happy and it's not going to affect the band. Girls Aloud is the most important thing.

SARAH: My main passion is music and I know I still have a lot to give and a lot to prove when it comes to my vocals. At the same time I don't want to pigeon-hole myself and be seen just as a singer. There are other things I love to do. I'm a keen horse-rider, I'd love to do presenting and acting. I did a bit of modelling but I think the underwear thing had its shelf life. It was good fun, really nice, but I'm not a glamour model and I just kind of outgrew it.

I had a cameo in a film, *Bad Day*, which was a nice step up the ladder for me. It's hard to break into acting when you're known for something else but sometimes it's who you know, and my cousin was producing the film. I still had to screen-test for the director, which was fine, and they wrote a small part for me. I suppose I'm more relaxed in front of cameras now, but because I'm trying to prove myself I tend to overact and run around like a bull in a china shop. Holding it down was the hardest part really.

I loved playing polo in *Passions*; going to Argentina was magical. I definitely want to go back one day. I'm so not a morning person but I was up early every day and you feel at the end of the day you've earned your rest, you deserve to sit down in front of the fire with a glass of red wine. I was just annoyed that I baled out in the last two minutes of the programme, but I had to jump because I was going to get trampled on. To be fair, the odds were stacked against me because we were in a smaller arena where there's a lot more turning, I didn't have any experience on sand and I hadn't ridden the horse until the day before. Then I ended up hitting my head and I was disorientated and embarrassed; the final two minutes – can you believe it? I got really emotional, more tears of frustration than anything. It was a hard thing but I'm glad I did it because it's going to stay with me forever.

KIMBERLEY: I went through an audition to sing in *Les Mis* in the West End in 2007 for *Passions* and it made me start thinking that doing musicals might be something I could think about way in the future. It was good to do and I learned a lot, but it just got harder and harder as I went further along the line. I didn't think I'd be doing anything so difficult; I just kind of ended up there. At first I was thinking, oh God, why am I putting myself out there when I don't need to? I don't need to be feeling like this again. I felt like I'd gone right back in time and was starting all over again, trying to get through an audition and be accepted, and I did feel the pressure. I think it's harder when you're known for something than when you're anonymous, but in a weird way it was a good thing to throw myself out of my comfort zone and into the deep end. I knew it was serious and that I had to come through somehow. Before I went on to do my solo I felt terrible – terrible, terrible. I'd been chatting to the cast and all of a sudden I felt violently ill and my heart started banging and I was thinking, my God, the song's so controlled and soft and quiet I'll not be able to get it out. I was going through all these techniques I'd been given to hold it together, taking a really short breath and letting it out slowly because it brings your heart rate back, but I didn't know if it was working because I still felt so nervous. Until I went on and opened my mouth I didn't know what would come out, whether I'd just be croaking. When I got the first line out I just thought, thank God. The rest was a bit of a blur. There were people crying and I got so many nice messages it was quite overwhelming. I think people just like to experience a journey with you.

NICOLA: Doing *Passions* was amazing. I've always been creative and strong-minded but I've never had the opportunity to show people that side of me. I got to create the Dainty Doll make-up range and it gave me a real sense of achievement because I was the boss. It was me making the decisions and my opinion that was valued. I do get that sense of achievement with Girls Aloud, but it's not all my effort. There are people around us, and the other four girls, all adding to the formula, so it's good to do your own thing sometimes. The last thing you want to feel is caged, that there's no opportunity to be the creative person you are. Doing the make-up range came naturally to me because I knew what I wanted and I trust my own judgement. I loved the whole experience – from designing the packaging to picking the right textures and colours and putting my own show together.

KIMBERLEY: I'm at a point in my life where I'm really happy, quite settled, not feeling worried about our career any more, not like I have in the past. I get to do an amazing job, something

I'm happy to wake up and do every day, and I just feel so lucky. I sometimes think, why have I got all this? Was this just how it was all planned? It was never that easy for me growing up, so to be in this position now is weird after getting knocked back and having odd bits of success here and there. Six years down the line with Girls Aloud I just feel like, my God, this was meant to be, that all the hard work and upset and disappointment was worth it. I even have that excited-about-life feeling all the time – you know when you just drift off and think: I'm so happy? It's a good place to be.

NICOLA: I love being in Girls Aloud: the photo shoots, all of it. I'm excited to come to work every day. I wouldn't change being in the band for anything. I totally appreciate everything and take it all in – even getting up at 4 a.m. for *GMTV*. Whatever happens we've had an amazing journey, over six years so far, and we've probably had more life experience and happiness in that time than some people have in a lifetime. My life IS Girls Aloud now. It's not just a job; it's the reason you are who you are, that you've got the friends you have, the house you have, the car you have. It's not like I have a job and my personal life is something else, something separate: it's all one whole. Before, I was trying to be two different people, but now I'm the same person at home and at work, and it's a lot easier. I can't actually believe I've been able to achieve my dream. I can't believe everything that's happened over the past six years. It's been madness, weird, amazing, unreal – every scenario it could be, it's been. But I love it; it's exciting and I feel at home in the band. It's been my home since I left home at 17.

NADINE: I would never be into splitting up. I don't think we should ever break up, I really don't. I think we should allow each person to do things individually – go off and have a baby, lie on the beach, whatever – but still remain Girls Aloud. Being in the band has completely changed my life. I've learned so many skills and had so many opportunities to see the world, and just being with the girls has been brilliant. I couldn't ask for four better girls. We all have the same idea about the band, where we want to go and what we want to do, and the fact we get on and have a laugh together is a bonus. Girl bands usually implode, but we've all had normal upbringings, none of us were showbiz kids, and we're close to our families, so we're all still very much attached to our own realities.

CHERYL: As far as the other girls go, it's totally fate. It could have been disastrous, five girls together, but we all have genuine respect for each other. We've been through so much, watched each other grow and learned from each other. All we had was each other and there wasn't any room for squabbling over stuff like who had the best dress; we're not like that anyway. In the beginning we were all learning about each other and changing. You just get an understanding. We all learned what made each other laugh, what helped in times of heartache or whatever, and we've got that solidarity now. I feel very fortunate and I never take any of it for granted because I always have this thing in the back of my mind that one day I'm going to wake up back in Newcastle, in the house I left, still 19, and it will all have been a crazy dream.

SARAH: This is my dream. I could never see myself doing anything else. It's all I've ever wanted and I feel like I've achieved so much, so much more than I'd ever have imagined. Anything else now would be a bonus.

NADINE: I totally think life turns out how it's meant to, that God guides you and picks what's right and wrong for you. It's a matter of you going along with it and trying to be a good person and make the right decisions, but ultimately I think your path is preordained. If something's not meant for you, you won't get it, simple as that. I think if you put your faith in God it takes a lot of pressure off. He wants you to be happy. I also think God will not throw something you can't handle at you.

NICOLA: Everything does happen for a reason, it can't all be coincidence. Like, my God, how am I in this position? It could have been the girl two doors down who's got a good voice as well but it's not – it's me. And I'm extremely grateful.

KIMBERLEY: I believe that things are meant for you. I was auditioning from such a young age and I went through a period of getting so close that I could have got disheartened, but I've just kept working hard and ended up with an opportunity that far outweighed anything I could have wished for. Being in Girls Aloud is my life but I still sit regularly and think this is so weird. It's what I wanted to do and dreamed about and secretly hoped would happen, and it has, but I think: how come it happened to me? There are so many amazing performers who keep trying and never get there, and for whatever reason I've been lucky enough to be given this experience so I have to embrace it and make the most of it. It's a brilliant place to be and I do feel very lucky. And the girls – there were hundreds of girls at those auditions I never spoke two words to, but I remember the other four from the beginning. Why did I get to know the ones who ended up in the band? Maybe it was meant to be and that's why it worked.

Q What's next for you and Girls Aloud?

KIMBERLEY: As we write this we're recording a new album and it's so exciting to be in that position. We don't know what else might happen for us, we're being offered so many amazing opportunities. I just want to make the most of every minute and keep enjoying being in the group, being with the girls, and living this life. It's been amazing so far and I'd love to think it can continue for a few more years at least.

NICOLA: We've just started recording the new album and we're getting to do lots of writing. I'm excited to be starting from scratch, creating something, seeing what kind of music we come up with this time. I'm a very ambitious person, very career-minded, and I'll try my hand at whatever comes my way. If Girls Aloud ended tomorrow I wouldn't feel like I could just settle down and have a family yet. I'm only 22 and where I'm at now I want to concentrate on my career and push myself with that, but I definitely want to be in love, get married and have kids one day.

NADINE: It's been six years so far and I've come a long way and experienced a lot through Girls Aloud, and I'll always be thankful for that. I've been able to branch out and do other things I'm interested in outside the music industry – like opening a family bar in California and getting into property. In the years to come I just want to continue on the good path I'm trying to get on: spending quality time with my family and friends and the girls, being the best person I can be, living life to the full. If that means recording another 10 albums or touring for an entire year, that's great, so be it. I love singing and I always see some form of singing being part of my life, even if it's just in our bar. As long as my family and friends are happy and healthy, that's what's important. I'm in a really good place in my life now where everything is exactly how I want it to be, and if I can stay as happy as I am now I'll be very thankful.

CHERYL: What's next for me is a family, hopefully. It's becoming a priority. I feel I've achieved a lot, I'm happy, and I think sometimes lifestyle can take over and cloud the important things in life. I started to think more about having children when I met Ashley, and especially when I got married, because it's naturally the next thing. These days there's no reason why you can't have a family and a career. I want my mother and Ashley's mother to be involved and I know that the longer I leave it the older they'll be and I want them to be able to enjoy being grandparents. I'm from a big

family and I want a big family, and that means I have to make a start soon – so watch this space.

SARAH: We've got loads lined up, another year of stuff coming up with Girls Aloud – we're busy with another album. We're all feisty and outspoken but we're very passionate and dedicated, and I think that's what's pulled us through. And we've been so lucky to have a team that's believed in us. We've definitely been through our ups and downs, but they've made us stronger, and for that we're really grateful.

I'm so ambitious and I really want to achieve a lot. I've done some acting, a bit of modelling, but the band is always going to be my priority. This is my baby. There are some days I think, 'I've had enough, I want a holiday' – but then I miss it. I do want to do more writing. I've been getting into my garage band on my Mac, doing my own songs and stuff, so I'm just starting to venture into making my own music and we'll see how I go with that. On the personal side, me and Tommy are moving to Buckinghamshire, hopefully, so it's all looking good at the moment. Once the cats have settled in I want to get a French bulldog. No horses yet, but give me time.

I don't want mega-fame, I just want to maintain a certain level of normality and be comfortable and successful. The only thing I do wish is that sometimes I could have an invisibility switch so I could just go about my day-to-day life, nip to the shops in my pyjamas or whatever, and not worry about being seen.

INDEX